cooking
moroccan

cooking
moroccan

Tess Mallos

THUNDER BAY
P·R·E·S·S

San Diego, California

contents

alluring aromas and flavors

The cooking of Morocco has a fascinating pedigree. While the cooking of the indigenous Berbers has always been a constant and a basis for the creation of new recipes, the ancestry of Moroccan cooking also includes Arabic, Persian, and Andalusian influences. How these inputs melded and created Moroccan cuisine is a matter of history.

The Arabs spread across North Africa under the banner of Islam and, with the Berbers, invaded the Iberian Peninsula (today's Spain and Portugal) in 711, dominating the region over the next seven centuries. The invaders were known as the Moors, after the Mauri, the Berber people of Maghreb (northwest Africa).

The Arabs named the peninsula Al Andaluz and introduced the cultivation of the saffron crocus, various citrus fruits, almonds, rice, and sugarcane, as well as the use of spices. These subsequently filtered down to Morocco. The full extent of Arabic culture, learning, medicine, cooking, architecture, and agriculture took flower in Al Andaluz, mirroring that which was flourishing in the courts of the caliphs of Baghdad, who in turn had learned so much from the Persians. This was the era of *A Thousand and One Arabian Nights*, a time when cookbooks were written and food was extolled in poetry.

From the eleventh century to the thirteenth century, the Berber dynasties of the Almoravides and the Almohades ruled in Al Andaluz and Morocco. The lavish court kitchens of Fez, Rabat, Meknes, and Marrakesh were the conduit by which new foods were introduced and recipes refined, a process that continued with later Berber dynasties.

What has evolved is a cuisine that is unique—one that makes the most of the ingredients it produces in abundance. This is evident in the dishes that use fruit for the sweet and sour flavors they impart, a Persian influence introduced by the Arabs, evolving into dishes that can only be Moroccan.

The Berbers' most important contribution to Morocco's cooking is couscous, the light and elegant grain regarded as the pasta of the Maghreb. Wheaten couscous is made into pellets with semolina grains and flour; however, cracked barley and maize are also used as a couscous.

While many of the Berber customs continue, such as their *moussems*— festivals and pilgrimages—held in vast tent cities erected for the occasion, the overriding culture is strongly intertwined with Islam. There is a strong sense of family, with all members present for the midday meal, and of hospitality, where a visitor is welcomed and given food or refreshment. During Ramadan, when Muslims fast for thirty days during the daylight hours, and other festivals of the Muslim year, food and family are an integral part of these times of religious observance.

For any meal, there are rules to follow. Hands must be washed; at a formal gathering, a servant or young family member circulates with a pitcher of warm, rose-scented water, a basin, and a towel. On a round table, food is served on a central platter or tagine, or in shallow dishes for easily picking up with the fingers. Morsels of food are picked from the communal dish with the thumb and first two fingers of the right hand and popped into the mouth, with diners taking food from the sections of the dishes nearest them. Hands are washed again at the end of the meal before diners retire to the reception room for mint tea and pastries.

Street food is very much part of daily life in Moroccan cities and towns. There are the ever-present kabob sellers, who grill lamb, liver, or kefta (ground lamb) on charcoal grills, ready to be slipped into a wedge of Moroccan bread. In coastal cities, fish is grilled on charcoal or fried in a golden batter and presented with crisp fried eggplant and potato. Hot chickpeas are served in paper cones with cumin and salt. The doughnut seller, with his cauldron of oil, shapes and fries crisp circles of dough.

In the cities, cafés cater to tourists, serving breakfasts of baguettes, bread with butter and jam, or yeast pancakes, as well as lunches of tagines, salads, kabobs, and couscous (although sandwiches and pizza are also available).

However, the best Moroccan food is that which is cooked in the home. The women are the cooks, the custodians of the recipes that are handed down from mother to daughter, with each cook making her own changes to suit her family's tastes and her own. No recipe books are needed—all is memorized to be passed on to the next generation of women. One could say that Moroccan food is a work in progress, as modern women take advantage of change. Where a mother might have insisted on cooking in a *tagine slaoui* (an earthenware cooking pot for stews), a daughter might work outside the home and save time by using a pressure cooker to make the same dish. Whatever the method, the ingredients used, the resulting delectable mélange of flavors and textures represents an indisputably Moroccan dish that has withstood the test of time. The recipes here aim to provide newcomers with a feel for this wonderful cuisine, exploring the ingredients, flavors, and smells that are so unique to Morocco.

little dishes

Morocco's little dishes, *mukabalatt*, like the antipasti of Italy, are served to whet the appetite before the main course. However, some are usually left on the table to accompany the main meal, especially the vegetables and salads. Even in the most humble household, three or four of these dishes are prepared. For a larger gathering, up to twenty different dishes are placed in the center of the low, round table—an artist's palette of colors to entice diners.

Spicy, jamlike dips of eggplant or tomato contrast creamy white *bessara*, cooked carrot or beet vegetable salads spiced with cumin, okra cooked in a tomato sauce, a cooked salad of wild herbs spiked with chili and garlic, and squash or sweet potato cubes simmered in chermoula—the versatile, spicy, herbed mixture that is so very Moroccan. Little dishes of meat and fish can also fill the table—small kabobs of grilled lamb and liver spiced with cumin, warm salads of brain or liver, fried stuffed sardines. *Briouats*, crisp fried pastries, enclose fillings of lamb, fish, shrimp, or the lemony egg and chicken filling used for *bisteeya*.

The distinguishing aspect of the Moroccan *mukabalatt* is the array of jewel-like, cooling, refreshing salads made of their famous oranges, as well as carrots, luscious red tomatoes, red-skinned radishes, scarlet beets, crisp cucumbers, fennel bulbs, sweet or hot bell peppers, and sweet red onions.

It is the combinations of these ingredients and their embellishments that set the little dishes apart, making them essentially Moroccan. A sprinkling of orange flower water here, a dusting of cinnamon or paprika there, a sprinkling of parsley, cilantro or mint leaves, dates, or raisins to add sweetness to the sour pieces of tangy preserved lemon rind—such transformations are made on a whim. A cucumber salad might be flavored with a wild herb called *za'atar* (a Moroccan herb similar to lemon thyme, which can be used instead) and speckled with black olives, or combined with the tang of lemon juice, the sweetness of sugar, and the perfume of orange flower water.

Then there are olives—little dishes of cured olives in their varied hues, unadorned or marinated in harissa, chermoula, or other concoctions, glistening and inviting. And olive oil—anointing vegetables and salads where its flavor enhances and emphasizes the taste of the ingredients on the palate.

Finally, no spread of little dishes is complete without bread—used to scoop up mouthfuls of dips and shredded salads, or to soak up flavorful dressings.

fava bean dip . . . . serves 6

KNOWN AS *BESSARA*, THIS DIP CAN ALSO BE MADE INTO A SOUP. COOK UNTIL THE BEANS ARE TENDER, PURÉE THEM, AND RETURN THEM TO THE PAN WITH THE REMAINING INGREDIENTS. ADD WATER TO GIVE A THICK SOUPY CONSISTENCY. HEAT UNTIL BOILING AND SERVE SPRINKLED WITH CHOPPED PARSLEY, PAPRIKA, AND CUMIN.

fava beans (dried or ready-skinned dried)	1 cup
garlic	2 cloves, crushed
ground cumin	1/2 teaspoon
lemon juice	2 tablespoons
olive oil	up to 1/3 cup
paprika	a large pinch
Italian parsley	3 tablespoons chopped
flatbread	to serve

Put the fava beans in a bowl, cover with 2 cups cold water, and leave to soak. If using dried beans with skins, soak for 24 hours, changing the water once. If using preskinned dried beans, soak them for 12 hours.

Drain the beans. If using beans with skins, remove the skins (slit the skins with the point of a knife and slip out the bean). Put the beans in a large saucepan with water; cover and bring to a boil. Once boiled, simmer covered over low heat for 1 hour or until tender (if the water boils over, uncover the pan a little). Remove the lid and cook for 15 minutes or until most of the liquid has evaporated.

Purée the beans in a food processor and then transfer to a bowl. Stir in the garlic, cumin, and lemon juice. Add salt to taste. Gradually stir in enough oil to give a spreadable or thick dipping consistency. If the mixture thickens as it cools, stir in a little warm water. Spread the bean purée over a large dish and sprinkle the paprika and parsley on the top. Serve with the flatbread.

Fava beans have been a staple food of the region for millennia—especially the dried beans, as they keep for many months. These require lengthy soaking so that the leathery skin can be removed, which results in the best flavor and a creamy white purée. Because this is time-consuming, it is possible to purchase preskinned dried fava beans that only require overnight soaking. Fresh fava beans are used when in season, the young beans added to tagines with the skin on; when more mature, the beans are blanched and skinned before cooking.

marinated olives......................................makes 3 cups

WHEREVER OLIVES ARE SOLD, MARINATED OLIVES ARE DISPLAYED ALONGSIDE THE GREEN AND BLACK VARIETIES, WITH A LITTLE MORE ADDED TO THE PRICE TAG FOR THE EXTRA INGREDIENTS. PREPARING THEM AT HOME IS SIMPLE, WITH DELICIOUS RESULTS.

preserved lemon olives

preserved lemon	1/2
red chili	1/2 teaspoon finely chopped
ground cumin	1/2 teaspoon
cilantro	3 tablespoons finely chopped leaves
Italian parsley	3 tablespoons finely chopped
garlic	2 cloves, finely chopped
lemon juice	3 tablespoons
olive oil	1/2 cup
cured green olives (whole or cracked)	3 cups

harissa olives

red bell pepper	1 (or 3 tablespoons chopped roasted bell pepper)
harissa	2 teaspoons
garlic	2 cloves, finely chopped
olive oil	1/2 cup
black olives, such as Kalamata	2 2/3 cups

To make the preserved lemon olives, rinse the preserved lemon under cold running water. Remove the pulp and membrane and rinse the rind. Drain and pat dry with paper towels. Chop the lemon rind very finely and place in a bowl along with the chili, cumin, cilantro, parsley, garlic, and lemon juice. Stir well and beat in the olive oil.

Rinse the green olives under cold running water and drain thoroughly. Add to the preserved lemon marinade, toss, and transfer to clean jars.

To make the harissa olives, first roast the bell pepper (skip this step if you are using roasted bell pepper). Cut the bell pepper into quarters, removing the seeds and white membrane. Lay the pieces as flat as possible, placing them skin side up under a hot broiler, and broil until the skin blisters and blackens. Turn and roast for 2–3 minutes on the fleshy side. Place the pieces in a plastic bag, tucking in the end of the bag to allow them to steam for 15 minutes. Remove the blackened skin, rinse and drain the bell pepper pieces, and then pat dry with paper towels. Finely chop one of the pieces—you will need 3 tablespoons in total. (Use the remainder in salads.) In a bowl, combine the chopped bell pepper with the harissa and garlic, and beat in the olive oil.

Rinse the black olives under cold running water and drain thoroughly. Add to the harissa marinade, toss, and transfer to clean jars.

Seal and refrigerate for 1–2 days before using. Bring the olives to room temperature 1 hour before serving. Use the preserved lemon-marinated olives within 5 days and the harissa-marinated olives within 10 days.

preserved lemons

Make preserved lemons with ripe, new-season fruit. The firmer the lemon, the more recently it has been picked. Store-bought lemons are usually coated with a wax, which has to be removed by scrubbing with a soft-bristled brush and warm water.

If the lemons are very firm, soak them in water for three days, changing the water daily. Wash the lemons if soaking is not required. Have wide-necked sterilized jars with plastic lids on hand. Cut the lemons from the stem end into quarters, almost to the base. Insert 4 teaspoons rock salt into each lemon, closing them up and placing them in a jar. Repeat until the jar is filled, sprinkling 1 tablespoon of salt between the layers. Pack the lemons into the jars as tightly as possible and add a bay leaf and a few black peppercorns to each jar if desired.

Juice more lemons and fill the jars, or add the juice of 1 lemon to each jar and fill with boiling water. Put the washed skin from a squeezed-out lemon half on top so that if any white mold forms (which is harmless), the skin and mold can be discarded when the jar is opened. Seal and store in a cool, dark place for four weeks, gently shaking the jars daily for the first week to dissolve the salt. The cloudy liquid clears in this time. Preserved lemons will keep for six months or more.

To prepare the lemons for cooking, remove a lemon from the jar with a fork. Separate the lemon into quarters and rinse it under cold running water. Remove and discard the pulp (you can add it to dishes, if you wish, but use it sparingly, as it has a bitter taste). Rinse the rind, pat dry with paper towels, and finely slice. Seal and refrigerate the jars once they have been opened.

lamb kabobs . . . . serves 4

WIDELY SOLD AS STREET FOOD WITH MOROCCAN BREAD, THESE SPICY LAMB KABOBS ARE ALSO OFTEN SERVED AS A LITTLE DISH. THE MEAT IS CUT INTO SMALL CUBES AND MARINATED BEFORE BEING THREADED ONTO BAMBOO OR METAL SKEWERS AND GRILLED.

boneless leg of lamb	1 lb. 10 oz.
onion	1, grated
paprika	1 teaspoon
ground cumin	1 teaspoon
Italian parsley	3 tablespoons finely chopped
olive oil	1/4 cup

harissa and tomato sauce

tomatoes	2
onion	1/2, grated for 3 tablespoons
olive oil	4 teaspoons
harissa	1 teaspoon or to taste (or 1/4 teaspoon cayenne pepper)
sugar	1/2 teaspoon

Soak eight bamboo skewers in water for 2 hours or use metal skewers. Do not trim the fat from the lamb. Cut the meat into 1 1/4-inch cubes and put it in a bowl. Add the onion, paprika, cumin, parsley, olive oil, and a generous grind of black pepper. Toss well to coat, then cover and marinate in the refrigerator for at least 2 hours.

To make the harissa and tomato sauce, halve the tomatoes horizontally and squeeze out the seeds. Coarsely grate the tomatoes into a bowl down to the skin, discarding the skin. In a saucepan, cook the onion in the olive oil for 2 minutes, stir in the harissa or cayenne pepper, and add the grated tomatoes, sugar, and 1/2 teaspoon salt. Cover and simmer for 10 minutes, then remove the lid and simmer for an additional 4 minutes or until the sauce reaches a thick, pouring consistency. Transfer to a bowl.

Thread the lamb cubes onto the skewers, leaving a little space between the meat cubes. Heat the barbecue grill to high and cook for 5–6 minutes, turning and brushing with the marinade. Alternatively, cook in a charbroil pan or under the broiler.

Serve the kabobs with the sauce; alternatively, omit the sauce and serve the kabobs with small dishes of ground cumin and salt on the side, to be added according to individual taste.

Leave any visible fat on the boneless leg of lamb.

Use a sharp knife to cut the lamb into large cubes.

Thread the marinated lamb cubes onto skewers.

kefta briouats..makes 12

THESE CIGAR-SHAPED PASTRIES ARE IDEAL FOR SERVING AS APPETIZERS, PERFECT FOR PICKING UP WITH THE FINGERS. USUALLY THEY ARE FRIED, BUT WITH PHYLLO PASTRY USED IN PLACE OF THE TRADITIONAL *WARKHA* PASTRY, THIS VERSION IS BAKED—MUCH EASIER TO COOK AND A GOOD DEAL HEALTHIER.

olive oil	4 teaspoons
onion	1 small, finely chopped
lean ground lamb	12 oz.
garlic	2 cloves, crushed
ground cumin	2 teaspoons
ground ginger	1/2 teaspoon
paprika	1/2 teaspoon
ground cinnamon	1/2 teaspoon
saffron threads	a pinch, soaked in a little warm water
harissa	1 teaspoon or to taste
cilantro	3 tablespoons chopped leaves
Italian parsley	3 tablespoons chopped
egg	1
phyllo pastry	6–8 sheets
butter	6 tablespoons, melted
sesame seeds	4 teaspoons

Heat the oil in a large frying pan, add the onion, and cook over low heat for 5 minutes or until the onion is soft. Increase the heat, add the lamb and garlic, and cook for 5 minutes, breaking up any lumps with the back of a wooden spoon. Add the spices, saffron water, harissa, and the chopped cilantro and parsley. Season to taste and cook for 1 minute, stirring to combine.

Transfer the lamb mixture to a sieve and drain to remove the fat. Put the mixture in a bowl and allow to cool slightly. Mix in the egg.

If the pastry is shorter than 15 1/2 inches in length, you will need extra sheets. Stack on a cutting surface. With a ruler and sharp knife, measure the length of the pastry and cut across the width to make strips 5 inches wide and 11–12 inches long. You will need 24 strips in all. Stack the phyllo in the folds of a dry dish towel or cover with plastic wrap to prevent it from drying out.

Put a strip of phyllo on a work surface with the narrow end toward you and brush with warm, melted butter. Top with another strip of phyllo and brush with melted butter. Place 4 teaspoons of filling 1/2 inch in from the base and sides of the strip. Fold the end of the phyllo over the filling, fold in the sides, and roll to the end of the strip. Place the seam side down on a greased cookie sheet. Repeat with the remaining ingredients. Brush the rolls with melted butter and sprinkle with the sesame seeds.

Preheat the oven to 350°F. It is best to do this after the rolls are completed so that the kitchen remains cool during shaping. Bake the *briouats* for 15 minutes or until lightly golden. Serve hot.

Brush a few pastry strips at a time with melted butter.

Put some filling on each pastry strip and roll up.

three ways with olives

OLIVES ARE OF SUCH IMPORTANCE IN THE MOROCCAN KITCHEN THAT MANY CITY STALLS AND STORES ARE STOCKED EXCLUSIVELY WITH THESE DELECTABLE PRESERVES. THEY ARE PICKED AT VARIOUS STAGES OF RIPENESS: GREEN AND PLUMP, PALER GREEN WITH A ROSY BLUSH, WINE RED, PURPLE BLACK, AND FINALLY BLACK AND BEGINNING TO SHRIVEL. ALL HUES MELLOW OR INTENSIFY IN THE CURING PROCESS. GREEN OLIVES ARE CRACKED BETWEEN TWO STONES TO EXPOSE THE FLESH IN CURING AND TO ALLOW FLAVORS TO PENETRATE IN COOKING.

cucumber and olive salad

Wash 4 short cucumbers and dry with paper towels. Do not peel the cucumbers if the skin is tender. Coarsely grate the cucumbers, mix with 1/2 teaspoon salt, and leave to drain well. Add 1 finely chopped red onion and 1 tablespoon superfine sugar to the cucumber and toss together. Beat 4 teaspoons red wine vinegar with 1/4 cup olive oil in a small bowl, then add 1 teaspoon finely chopped lemon thyme and freshly ground black pepper to taste. Whisk the ingredients together and pour over the cucumber. Cover and chill for 15 minutes. Sprinkle with 1/2 cup black olives and serve with flatbread. Serves 4.

warm olives with lemon and herbs

Rinse 2 cups cured cracked green or black Kalamata olives, drain, and place in a saucepan with enough water to cover. Bring to a boil and cook for 5 minutes, then drain in a sieve. Add 1/3 cup olive oil and 1 teaspoon fennel seeds to the saucepan and heat until fragrant. Add 2 finely chopped garlic cloves, the drained olives, a pinch of cayenne pepper, and the finely shredded zest and juice of 1 lemon. Toss for 2 minutes or until the olives are hot. Transfer to a bowl and toss with 4 teaspoons each of finely chopped cilantro leaves and Italian parsley. Serve hot with crusty bread to soak up the juices. Serves 4.

fennel and olive salad

Wash 2 fennel bulbs and remove the outer layers if they are wilted or damaged. Cut off the stems and slice thinly across the bulb to the base, discarding the base. Place the sliced fennel in a shallow bowl and sprinkle 3/4 cup black olives on top. Beat 3 tablespoons lemon juice with 1/3 cup extra-virgin olive oil in a pitcher. Season to taste and add 3 tablespoons finely chopped Italian parsley. If desired, add 1 teaspoon finely chopped, seeded red chili. Beat well and pour over the fennel and olives just before serving. Toss lightly. Serves 4.

briouats with seafood .... makes 24

WHEN MAKING SMALL PASTRIES USING PHYLLO, THE LESS THE PASTRY IS HANDLED THE BETTER. STACK THE SHEETS AND CUT THE STRIPS AS DIRECTED; A CRAFT KNIFE IS EXCELLENT FOR CUTTING THROUGH THE STACK. AVOID USING A DAMP DISH TOWEL, AS IT CAN RUIN THE PHYLLO.

filling

boneless white fish fillets	9 oz. (or 7 oz. cooked, shelled shrimp)
Italian parsley	3 tablespoons finely chopped
scallion	4 teaspoons finely chopped
garlic	1 clove, crushed
paprika	1/2 teaspoon
ground cumin	1/4 teaspoon
cayenne pepper	a pinch
lemon juice	4 teaspoons
olive oil	4 teaspoons
phyllo pastry	6 sheets
egg white	1, lightly beaten
oil	for deep-frying
superfine sugar	1/4 cup
cayenne pepper	1/8 teaspoon
ground cinnamon	1 teaspoon

To make the filling, first poach the fish gently by covering it in lightly salted water until the flesh flakes—about 4–5 minutes. Remove from the poaching liquid to a plate and cover closely with plastic wrap so that the surface does not dry as it cools. When cool, flake the fish. If using shrimp, cut them into small pieces. Put the fish or shrimp in a bowl and add the parsley, scallion, garlic, paprika, cumin, cayenne pepper, lemon juice, and olive oil. Toss well to mix.

Stack the phyllo sheets on a cutting board. With a ruler and sharp knife, measure and cut across the width of the pastry to make strips 5 inches wide and 11–12 inches long. You will need 24 strips. Stack the cut phyllo in the folds of a dry dish towel or cover it with plastic wrap to prevent it from drying out.

Take a phyllo strip and, with the narrow end toward you, fold it in half across its width to make a strip 2 1/2 inches wide. Place a generous teaspoon of filling 3/4 inch in from the base of the strip and fold the end diagonally across the filling so that the baselines up with the side of the strip, forming a triangle. Fold straight up once, then fold diagonally to the opposite side. Continue folding in this way until you near the end of the strip, then brush the phyllo lightly with egg white and complete the fold. Place seam side down on a cloth-covered tray. Cover with a dish towel until ready to fry. Work quickly, as the briouats are best cooked within 10 minutes of assembling.

Heat the oil to 350°F or until a cube of bread dropped into the oil browns in 15 seconds. Add four briouats at a time and fry until golden, turning to brown evenly. Remove with a slotted spoon and drain on paper towels. Serve hot, accompanied by a small bowl of sugar mixed with cayenne and cinnamon.

Fold the pastry over the filling to form a triangle.

Brush the end of the pastry with egg white and seal the triangle.

preserved lemon and tomato salad

WITH ITS HOT CLIMATE AND FERTILE LAND, MOROCCO PROVIDES TOMATOES THAT ARE RICHLY RED AND LUSCIOUS. THIS IS ONE OF THOSE SALADS THAT TEMPTS THE PALATE WITH ITS VARIED FLAVORS. SERVE IT AS AN APPETIZER IN THE MOROCCAN MANNER OR AS AN ACCOMPANIMENT TO CHARBROILED CHICKEN OR LAMB.

tomatoes	6 medium
red onion	1
preserved lemon	1
olive oil	1/4 cup
lemon juice	4 teaspoons
paprika	1/2 teaspoon
Italian parsley	4 teaspoons finely chopped
cilantro	3 tablespoons finely chopped leaves

Peel the tomatoes by scoring a cross in the base of each one with a knife. Put the tomatoes in a bowl of boiling water for 20 seconds, then plunge them into a bowl of cold water to cool. Remove from the water and peel the skin away from the cross—it should slip off easily. Cut the tomatoes in half horizontally and squeeze out the seeds. Dice the tomatoes and put them in a bowl.

Halve the onion lengthwise, cut out the root end, slice into slender wedges, and add to the bowl.

Separate the preserved lemon into quarters, remove the pulp and membrane, and discard them. Rinse the rind, pat dry with paper towels, and cut into fine strips. Add to the onion and tomato.

Beat the olive oil, lemon juice, and paprika, and add 1/2 teaspoon salt and a good grinding of black pepper. Pour over the salad, toss lightly, and then cover and set aside for 30 minutes. Just before serving, add the parsley and cilantro and toss again.

Taste a sun-ripened tomato plucked straight from the vine and you have an indication of the perfect Moroccan tomato. These days, store-bought tomatoes are criticized for their lack of flavor and thick skins; tomato cultivars had to be developed to withstand long trips to markets. To improve the flavor of such tomatoes, let them ripen at room temperature if necessary, store in the refrigerator, and then bring to room temperature before using them in salads. If the skin is thick, remove it—there are two methods used in recipes. When used in cooking, some tomato paste and a little sugar improves the flavor.

three ways with carrots

ONE OF THE MOST POPULAR VEGETABLES FOR DELECTABLE APPETIZER SALADS IS THE HUMBLE CARROT. IT IS INEVITABLE THAT DISHES SHOULD REFLECT THE MOROCCANS' LOVE OF COLOR, AND THE CARROT IS APPRECIATED FOR ITS BRILLIANT HUE, AS WELL AS ITS SWEETNESS. MANY COOKS REMOVE THE CORES FROM CARROTS, ESPECIALLY WHEN CUTTING THEM INTO QUARTERS OR STICKS. INTERESTINGLY, THE ARABS INTRODUCED THE CARROT THROUGH THE MOORS TO EUROPE.

spiced carrots

Cut 4 medium carrots into 2½ x ½-inch sticks. Cook the carrots in boiling salted water for 10 minutes or until tender. Drain and toss lightly with ½ teaspoon paprika, ½ teaspoon ground cumin, 3 tablespoons finely chopped Italian parsley, 4 teaspoons lemon juice, and 3 tablespoons olive oil. Transfer to a serving bowl, cover, and chill for 2 hours for the flavors to develop. Season with salt. Serve warm or at room temperature. Serves 4.

orange and carrot salad

Wash and dry 3 sweet oranges, then cut off the tops and bases. Cut the peel off with a sharp knife, removing all traces of pith and cutting through the outer membranes to expose the flesh. One at a time, hold the oranges over a bowl to catch the juice and segment them by cutting between the membranes. Remove the seeds and put the segments in the bowl. Squeeze the remains of the oranges to extract all the juice. Pour the juice into another bowl. Peel and grate 4 medium carrots on the shredding side of the grater or use a julienne vegetable shredder. Alternatively, julienne the carrots with a sharp knife. Put the carrots in the bowl with the orange juice and add 3 tablespoons lemon juice, 1 teaspoon ground cinnamon, 4 teaspoons superfine sugar, a small pinch of salt, and 4 teaspoons orange flower water. Stir well to combine. Cover the carrot mixture and oranges and chill until required. Just before serving, drain off the accumulated juice from the oranges and arrange the segments around the edge of a serving dish. Pile the shredded carrots in the center and top with small mint leaves. Dust the oranges lightly with a little extra cinnamon. Serves 6.

carrot soup with spices

Using the shredding side of a grater, grate 4 medium carrots. Place 1 grated onion in a saucepan with 2 tablespoons butter and cook over medium heat for 3 minutes. Add 2 crushed garlic cloves, ½ teaspoon each of ground turmeric, ginger, cinnamon, paprika, and cumin, a pinch of cayenne pepper, and the grated carrot. Cook for a few seconds, then add 5 cups chicken stock. Bring to a boil, cover, and simmer over low heat for 15 minutes. Add ¼ cup couscous, stir until boiling, and then cover and simmer gently for an additional 20 minutes. Add 2 teaspoons lemon juice and serve hot, topped with a little chopped Italian parsley. Serves 4.

warm eggplant salad . . . . serves 6–8

THE INGREDIENTS OF THIS POPULAR AND TASTY MOROCCAN EGGPLANT SALAD, CALLED *ZEILOOK*, ARE COOKED. THIS DELICIOUS BLEND IS IDEAL SERVED AS A DIP WITH CRUSTY BREAD. EGGPLANT HAS NEVER TASTED SO GOOD.

eggplants	2
tomatoes	3 medium
olive oil	for frying
garlic	2 cloves, finely chopped
paprika	1 teaspoon
ground cumin	1/2 teaspoon
cayenne pepper	1/4 teaspoon or to taste
cilantro	3 tablespoons finely chopped leaves
lemon juice	3 tablespoons
preserved lemon	1/2, optional (or fresh lemon slices for serving)

Using a vegetable peeler, remove strips of skin along the length of each eggplant. Cut the eggplants into 1/2-inch-thick slices, sprinkle with salt, and layer in a colander. Leave for 20–30 minutes, then rinse under cold running water. Drain, squeeze the slices gently, and then pat them dry with paper towels.

Peel the tomatoes by first scoring a cross in the base of each one with a knife. Put in a bowl of boiling water for 20 seconds, then plunge into a bowl of cold water to cool. Remove from the water and peel the skin away from the cross—it should slip off easily. Cut the tomatoes in half horizontally and squeeze out the seeds. Chop the tomatoes and set aside.

Add the olive oil to a frying pan to a depth of 1/4 inch. Heat the oil and fry the eggplant slices in batches until they are browned on each side. Remove from the pan and set aside on a plate. Add more oil to the pan as needed.

Using the oil left in the pan, cook the garlic over low heat for a few seconds. Add the tomato, paprika, cumin, and cayenne pepper and increase the heat to medium. Add the eggplant slices and cook, mashing the eggplant and tomato gently with a fork. Continue to cook until most of the liquid has evaporated. When the oil separates, drain off some if it seems excessive; however, some oil should be left in as it adds to the flavor of the dish. Add the cilantro and lemon juice and season with freshly ground black pepper and a little salt if necessary. Tip into a serving bowl.

If using preserved lemon, rinse under cold running water and remove the pulp and membrane. Chop the rind into small pieces and sprinkle over the eggplant or, alternatively, garnish with slices of fresh lemon. Serve warm or at room temperature with bread.

Use a vegetable peeler to remove strips of skin from the eggplant.

stuffed sardines..serves 6

SARDINES ARE AT THEIR BEST WHEN SANDWICHED WITH A FILLING OF CHERMOULA. SOME FISH MERCHANTS SPLIT AND FILLET THEM, CUTTING OFF THE TAILS, BUT IT IS EASY TO DO THIS YOURSELF AND YOU CAN EVEN LEAVE THE TAILS ON FOR EFFECT.

fresh sardines	24 whole
olive oil	for frying
all-purpose flour	for coating
lemon wedges	to serve

stuffing

onion	4 teaspoons grated and drained
garlic	1 clove, crushed
Italian parsley	¼ cup finely chopped
cilantro	¼ cup finely chopped leaves
cayenne pepper	¼ teaspoon
paprika	½ teaspoon
freshly ground black pepper	¼ teaspoon
ground cumin	½ teaspoon
lemon zest	½ teaspoon grated
lemon juice	2 teaspoons
olive oil	2 teaspoons

To butterfly the sardines, first remove the heads. Cut through the underside of the sardines and rinse under cold running water. Snip the backbone at the tail with kitchen scissors, without cutting through the skin, and pull carefully away from the body starting from the tail end. Open out the sardines, pat the inside surface dry with paper towels, and sprinkle lightly with salt. Set aside.

To make the stuffing, put the drained onion in a bowl and add the garlic, parsley, cilantro, cayenne pepper, paprika, black pepper, cumin, lemon zest, lemon juice, and olive oil. Mix well.

Place 12 sardines on the work surface, skin side down. Spread the stuffing evenly on each sardine and cover with another sardine, skin side up. Press them firmly together.

Add the olive oil to a large frying pan to a depth of ¼ inch and heat. Coat the sardines with flour and fry in the hot oil for 2 minutes on each side, until crisp and evenly browned. Serve hot with lemon wedges.

Spread the stuffing over the inner side of the sardines.

Cover the stuffing with another sardine, skin side up.

Fry the flour-coated sardines in hot oil until crisp and browned.

three ways with tomatoes

THE TOMATO, ONION, AND BELL PEPPER SALAD HERE MAKES THE MOST OF MOROCCO'S BEAUTIFUL TOMATOES AND IS THE MOST POPULAR SALAD SERVED IN MOROCCAN HOUSEHOLDS. THE SWEET TOMATO JAM IS A WINNING COMBINATION OF FLAVORS, SERVED AS A DIP WITH BREAD FOR AN APPETIZER, AS A BASIS FOR A LAMB TAGINE (PAGE 77), OR USED AS A STUFFING FOR FISH. IT IS TEMPTING TO USE CANNED TOMATOES FOR THE JAM, BUT FRESH TOMATOES GIVE A SUPERIOR FLAVOR.

okra with tomato sauce

Use 75 medium fresh okra or rinse and drain 1 lb. 12 oz. canned okra. Heat ¼ cup olive oil in a large frying pan over medium heat, add 1 chopped onion, and cook for 5 minutes or until golden. Add 2 crushed garlic cloves and cook for another minute. If using fresh okra, add and cook, stirring, for 4–5 minutes. Add 14-oz. can chopped tomatoes, 2 teaspoons sugar, and ¼ cup lemon juice and simmer, stirring occasionally, for 3–4 minutes. Stir in 1½ cups finely chopped cilantro and the canned okra, if using. Remove from the heat and serve. Serves 4–6.

tomato, onion, and bell pepper salad

Cut 2 green bell peppers into large, flattish pieces and remove the seeds and white membrane. Place the pieces skin side up under a hot broiler and broil until the skin blackens. Turn them over and cook for 2–3 minutes on the fleshy side. Place the pieces in a plastic bag, tucking in the end of the bag to steam until cool enough to handle. Remove the blackened skin and cut the flesh into short strips. Place in a bowl, along with 4 peeled, seeded, and diced tomatoes. Halve 1 red onion lengthwise, remove the root end, and cut into slender wedges. Add to the bowl, along with 1 finely chopped garlic clove and 4 teaspoons finely chopped Italian parsley. Beat ⅓ cup olive oil with 4 teaspoons red wine vinegar and add ½ teaspoon salt and a good grinding of black pepper. Pour the dressing over the salad and toss well. Serves 4.

sweet tomato jam

Halve 12 medium ripe tomatoes horizontally and squeeze out the seeds. Coarsely grate the tomatoes down to the skin into a bowl, discarding the skin. Heat ¼ cup olive oil in a heavy-based saucepan over low heat and add 2 coarsely grated onions. Cook for 5 minutes, then stir in 2 crushed garlic cloves, 1 teaspoon ground ginger, 1 cinnamon stick, and ¼ teaspoon freshly ground black pepper. Cook for about 1 minute. Add ¼ teaspoon ground saffron threads (if desired), ¼ cup tomato paste, and the grated tomatoes. Season with ½ teaspoon salt. Simmer uncovered over medium heat for 45–50 minutes or until most of the liquid evaporates, stirring often when the sauce starts to thicken to prevent it from catching on the base of the pan. When the oil begins to separate, stir in 3 tablespoons honey and 1½ teaspoons ground cinnamon and cook over low heat for 2 minutes. Adjust the seasoning with salt if necessary. Store in a clean, sealed jar in the refrigerator for up to one week. Makes 2½ cups.

tuna brik . . . . serves 2

THERE IS AN ART TO EATING THIS TUNISIAN SPECIALTY, WHICH IS ALSO POPULAR IN MOROCCO. HOLD THE BRIK BY THE CORNERS WITH THE FILLING SIDE UPWARD AND BITE INTO THE EGG, ALLOWING THE RUNNY YOLK TO ACT AS A SAUCE FOR THE FILLING.

onion	3 tablespoons finely chopped
olive oil	2 teaspoons
anchovy fillets	3, finely chopped
canned tuna in water	3½ oz.
capers	2 teaspoons, rinsed, drained, and chopped
Italian parsley	3 tablespoons finely chopped
oil	for frying
square egg roll skins	4 x 8½ inch
egg white	1, lightly beaten
eggs	4, small

In a small frying pan, gently cook the onion in the olive oil until softened. Add the anchovies and cook, stirring until the anchovies have melted. Tip into a bowl. Drain the tuna well and add to the bowl. Add the capers and parsley. Mix well, breaking up the chunks of tuna.

Pour the oil into a large frying pan to a depth of ½ inch and place over medium heat.

Put an egg roll skin on the work surface and brush the edge with beaten egg white. Put a quarter of the filling on one side of the skin, in a triangle shape, with the edge of the filling just touching the center of the skin. Make a well in the filling with the back of a spoon and break an egg into the center of the filling. Fold the skin over to form a triangle. Firmly press the edges together to seal.

As soon as you have finished the first pastry triangle, carefully lift it up using a wide spatula to help support the filling, and slide it into the hot oil. Fry for about 30 seconds on each side, spooning hot oil on top at the beginning of frying. If a firmly cooked egg is preferred, cook for 50 seconds on each side. When golden brown and crisp, remove with the spatula and drain on paper towels. Repeat with the remaining skins and filling. Do not be tempted to prepare all the pastry triangles before frying them, as the moist filling will soak through the skin.

Spread the filling on the wrapper and break an egg into the center.

Carefully fold the wrapper over the egg to form a triangle.

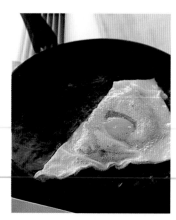
Cook the pastry triangles in hot oil until golden brown and crisp.

three ways with cumin

ONE OF THE MOST COMMONLY USED SPICES IN MOROCCAN COOKING, CUMIN CAN RAISE THE SIMPLEST FOODS TO NEW HEIGHTS. IT IS USED SPARINGLY IN COOKING AND IS OFTEN SERVED AS A CONDIMENT, ESPECIALLY WITH LAMB DISHES. SMALL DISHES OF CUMIN AND SALT ARE PLACED ON THE TABLE TO BE ADDED ACCORDING TO INDIVIDUAL TASTE. STREET FOOD STALL-HOLDERS HAND OUT PAPER PACKETS CONTAINING CUMIN AND SALT WITH LAMB, KEFTA, OR LIVER KABOBS, OR HARD-BOILED EGGS.

beet and cumin salad

Cut the stems from 6 medium-sized beets, leaving ³⁄4 inch attached. Do not trim the roots. Wash well to remove all traces of soil, then boil in salted water for 1 hour or until tender. Leave until cool enough to handle. In a deep bowl, beat ¹⁄3 cup olive oil with 4 teaspoons red wine vinegar, ¹⁄2 teaspoon ground cumin, and a good grinding of black pepper to make a dressing. Wearing rubber gloves so the beet juice doesn't stain your hands, peel the warm beets and trim the roots. Halve them, cut into slender wedges, and place in the dressing. Halve 1 red onion, slice it into slender wedges, and add to the beets. Add 3 tablespoons chopped Italian parsley and toss well. Serve warm or at room temperature. Serves 4–6.

eggplant jam

Cut 2 medium eggplants into ¹⁄2-inch-thick slices. Sprinkle with salt and drain in a colander for 30 minutes. Rinse well, squeeze gently, and pat dry. Heat about ¹⁄4 inch of olive oil in a large frying pan over medium heat and fry the eggplant in batches until it is golden brown on both sides. Drain on paper towels, then chop finely. Put the eggplant in a colander and leave it until most of the oil has drained off, then transfer it to a bowl and add 2 crushed garlic cloves, 1 teaspoon paprika, 1¹⁄2 teaspoons ground cumin, 3 tablespoons chopped cilantro, and ¹⁄2 teaspoon sugar. Wipe out the pan, add the eggplant mixture, and stir constantly over medium heat for 2 minutes. Transfer to a bowl, stir in 4 teaspoons lemon juice, and season. Serve at room temperature with bread as a dip, or with other salads. Serves 6–8.

liver kabobs

Soak eight bamboo skewers in water for 2 hours or use small metal skewers. Pull off the fine membrane covering a 1 lb. 2 oz. piece of lamb liver. Cut the liver into ³⁄4-inch-thick slices, then cut into cubes, removing any tubes from the liver as necessary. Put in a bowl and sprinkle with 1 teaspoon paprika, ¹⁄2 teaspoon ground cumin, ¹⁄4 teaspoon cayenne pepper, and 1 teaspoon salt. Add 3 tablespoons olive oil and toss well. Set aside for 5 minutes. Thread five or six pieces of liver onto each skewer, leaving a little space between the pieces. Cook on a barbecue grill or in a charbroil pan, brushing with any of the oil remaining in the bowl. Cook for about 1 minute each side—the liver should remain pink in the center, otherwise it will toughen. Serve the kabobs with a round of Moroccan bread or pita breads. If using Moroccan bread, cut the bread into quarters and slit each piece in half almost to the crust. For each serving, slide the liver from two skewers into the bread pocket. If using pita bread, do not split it; just slide the liver from the skewers onto the center and fold up the sides. Offer separate small dishes of ground cumin, coarse salt, and cayenne pepper on the side, or stir ¹⁄4 cup hot water into ¹⁄4 cup harissa and serve as a sauce. Serves 4.

merguez with bell pepper and onion..serves 4

CHARBROILED MERGUEZ SAUSAGE SERVED WITH FLAT MOROCCAN BREAD, FRIED BELL PEPPERS, AND ONIONS IS ONE OF THE DELIGHTS OF MOROCCAN STREET FOOD STALLS. IT IS ALSO SERVED AS AN APPETIZER—CUT THE COOKED SAUSAGE INTO BITE-SIZE PIECES, MIX WITH THE VEGETABLES, AND SERVE IN A SHALLOW BOWL.

merguez sausages	8
green bell peppers	2
red bell pepper	1
onion	1 large
olive oil	3 tablespoons
Moroccan bread	2 rounds (or pita breads to serve)

Prick the sausages with a fork, then cook on a barbecue grill over low to medium heat, turning frequently until cooked through—this will take about 8–10 minutes. Alternatively, cook the sausages in a charbroil pan.

Meanwhile, cut the bell peppers into quarters, remove the seeds and white membrane, and cut into strips about 1/2 inch wide. Halve the onion and slice thinly. Heat the olive oil in a frying pan on the barbecue, add the bell pepper strips and onion, and cook over medium heat, stirring often for about 10 minutes or until tender. If the onion begins to burn, reduce the heat to low or move the pan to a cooler section of the barbecue. Season with salt and freshly ground black pepper.

If serving with Moroccan bread, cut the rounds into quarters. Put the sausages and a generous amount of the bell pepper mixture in the bread or roll up in pita bread. Alternatively, serve the sausages on plates with the vegetables, and the bread on the side.

Fiery hot merguez sausage is a Tunisian specialty adopted by Moroccans, although their version is not as hot as the original. Made of lamb with a fair portion of lamb fat to give it moistness and succulence, it is hot and pungent with the addition of harissa (hot chili paste) and garlic, and flavored with ground fennel and coriander seeds, cumin, paprika, black pepper, and allspice. Gourmet butchers and delicatessens, as well as some Middle Eastern food markets, stock merguez. Traditionally a thin sausage, its length can vary.

the bakery

To a Moroccan, bread, or *khobz*, is sacred, to be revered, savored, and never wasted. *Kesra*, or country bread, is made every day in rural households, the dough mixed and kneaded in a shallow wooden or earthenware vessel called a *gsaa*. It is a simple bread, made with whole-wheat flour, usually mixed with unbleached flour and perhaps a handful of yellow cornmeal or barley flour. Only water, a little salt, and sugar are used in the dough, which is leavened with a sourdough starter kept from the previous day's baking (though often supplemented with dried yeast granules these days).

Shaped in flattish round loaves and placed on trays, the loaves are stamped with each household's own mark for identification, covered with a cloth, and left to rise only once. Aniseeds and sesame seeds are sometimes used to flavor the bread or are sprinkled over the top. The loaves are then taken on trays to the local bakery or baked in a communal oven—the marking on each loaf clearly identifying the owner.

These flattish loaves have a loose crumb that can absorb the sauce of the tagine, but are still crusty enough to support food as it is conveyed to the mouth with the fingers. The bread is cut into wedges and distributed by one person at the table—to prevent household quarrels. Flatter loaves are made for eating with kabobs, and baguettes (a legacy from the French) are baked in some bakeries and patisseries.

Other breads of the *bled*, or countryside, include a bread sheet called *therfist*, which is cooked on a pottery dome over embers. Another, made by the Tuaregs—the nomadic Berbers of the Sahara—is called *tagella* and is cooked on hot stones.

filled savory pancakes . . . . makes 12

THESE YEAST-DOUGH PANCAKES ARE FLAKY, LIGHT, AND CRISP AS A RESULT OF CAREFUL ROLLING AND FOLDING. THE SPICED KEFTA MIXTURE IS A SUBSTITUTE FOR A PRESERVED SPICED MEAT CALLED *KHLII*, TRADITIONALLY USED IN MOROCCO FOR THESE DELICIOUS SNACK BREADS.

active dried yeast	2 teaspoons
sugar	1 teaspoon
all-purpose flour	2³/4 cups
olive oil	for coating
oil	for frying

spiced kefta paste

smen or ghee	1/3 cup
finely ground beef	9 oz.
onion	3 tablespoons grated
garlic	4 cloves, finely chopped
ground cumin	2 teaspoons
ground coriander	2 teaspoons

Dissolve the yeast in 1/2 cup lukewarm water and stir in the sugar. Sift the flour and 1/2 teaspoon salt into a shallow bowl and make a well in the center. Pour the yeast mixture into the well, then add another 1/2 cup lukewarm water. Stir sufficient flour into the liquid to form a thin batter, cover the bowl with a cloth, and leave for 15 minutes until bubbles form. Gradually stir in the remaining flour, then mix with your hand until a sticky dough is formed. If it is too stiff, add a little more water. Knead for 10 minutes in the bowl until smooth and elastic. Pour a little olive oil down the side of the bowl, turn the ball of dough to coat in the oil, cover, and leave in a warm place for 30 minutes.

To make the spiced kefta, heat the smen or ghee in a frying pan, add the beef, and stir over high heat until browned. Reduce the heat to low, add the onion, garlic, cumin, and coriander, and season with salt and freshly ground black pepper. Cook for 2 minutes, stirring, then add 2 cups water. Cover and simmer for 30–45 minutes until the water evaporates and the fat separates. Tip into a food processor and process to a paste; alternatively, pound to a paste in a mortar. Set aside to cool.

Using oiled hands, punch down the dough and divide into twelve balls. Oil the work surface and a rolling pin and roll out and stretch a dough ball into a 7-inch round. Spread thinly with kefta paste. Fold the sides in so that they overlap, then fold in the other two sides to overlap in the center. Roll out and shape into a 3¹/2 x 5-inch rectangle. Place on an oiled tray and repeat with the remaining dough balls.

In a frying pan, add the oil to a depth of 1/2 inch. Place over high heat and, when almost smoking, reduce the heat to medium and add two pancakes. Cook for about 1 minute on each side or until browned and crisp and cooked through. Drain on paper towels and repeat with the remaining pancakes.

Roll out and stretch each portion of dough into a circle.

Fold the sides of the dough over the kefta paste.

moroccan bread

STORE ACTIVE DRIED YEAST IN THE REFRIGERATOR. IF PAST ITS USE-BY DATE, DISSOLVE ½ TEASPOON EACH OF THE YEAST AND SUGAR IN ¼ CUP WARM WATER AND LEAVE FOR 15 MINUTES. IF IT FROTHS, USE THE YEAST; OTHERWISE DISCARD IT AND PURCHASE A NEW BATCH.

active dried yeast	3 teaspoons
bread flour or all-purpose flour, preferably unbleached	4 cups
whole-wheat flour	1⅓ cups
milk	½ cup, lukewarm
cornmeal	3 tablespoons
whole aniseed, roasted sesame seeds, black sesame seeds, or coarse salt	4 teaspoons, optional

Dissolve the yeast in ½ cup lukewarm water. Sift the flours and 1½ teaspoons salt into a mixing bowl and make a well in the center. Pour the yeast mixture into the well, then add another 1 cup lukewarm water and the lukewarm milk. Stir sufficient flour into the liquid to form a thin batter, cover the bowl with a cloth, and leave for 15 minutes until bubbles form.

Gradually stir in the remaining flour, then mix with your hands to form a soft dough, adding a little extra water if necessary. Turn out onto a lightly floured work surface and knead for 10 minutes until smooth and elastic and the dough springs back when an impression is made with a fingertip. Only knead in extra all-purpose flour if the dough remains sticky after a few minutes of kneading.

As the dough requires only one rising, divide it into three equal-size pieces. Shape each piece into a ball and roll out on a lightly floured work surface to a 9-inch round (or a 10½-inch round for flatter breads).

Sift the cornmeal onto trays. Lift the rounds onto the trays, reshaping if necessary. Brush the tops lightly with water and, if desired, sprinkle with any one of the toppings, pressing it in lightly. Cover the loaves with dish towels and leave in a warm, draft-free place for 1 hour to rise. The bread has risen sufficiently when a depression remains in the dough after it is pressed lightly with a fingertip.

While the loaves are rising, preheat the oven to 425°F. Just before baking, prick the breads in several places with a fork. Put the breads in the hot oven and bake for 12–15 minutes or until they are golden and sound hollow when the base is tapped. Cool on a wire rack. Cut in wedges to serve. Use on the day of baking. Any leftover loaves may be frozen.

Knead the dough on a floured surface until smooth and elastic.

Lift the dough onto a tray and reshape if necessary.

a simple feast

Where there is lamb grilling over charcoal fires, aromas assail the senses. Moroccan bread, filled with tender cubes redolent with spices, is very inviting indeed. A simple feast, so typical of the street food that is served by the many stalls found in city squares and *souks*. The two most popular soups, *harira* and *bessara*, are ladled out of simmering cauldrons into pottery bowls. In the evenings, long tables laden with salads, tagines, and couscous tempt customers, who sit on benches and are served by white-garbed men.

In their homes, Moroccan women also prepare their own delicious meals. Using the most basic kitchen equipment, they have developed the cuisine to its present form. They cook with confidence—a pinch of this, a handful of that—just as their mothers have taught them, adding and changing according to their own family's preferences.

Onions, garlic, fresh herbs, and spices are staples of Moroccan cuisine, and lamb, chicken, chickpeas, and lentils are always available. However, the choice of vegetables and fruits added to tagines and stews is dictated by the seasons. In spring, tender young fava beans can be cooked whole or shelled, but will also need to be skinned when more mature. Spring to early summer brings fresh green peas, green beans, zucchini, wild artichokes, and eggplants. Tomatoes, cucumbers, and bell peppers are at their best in summer, with autumn heralding the arrival of turnips, quinces, the best oranges, apples, and pears. Beets, cauliflower, celery, and fennel bulbs are winter fare. Squash mature in winter but keep well. Pitted fruits, melons, and berries abound in summer, with other produce available year-round.

The woman of the household prepares the main meal, served at midday, and it is a family feast. Usually it features a tagine of lamb or chicken extended with the addition of chickpeas—or it could be a tagine of chickpeas or lentils; if it is Friday, couscous is cooked. The day's choice of vegetables and fruits dictate what is put in the tagine and which salad and vegetable dishes will be prepared. Cooking could be over a charcoal grill or a flame from a gas bottle, although gas cookers are increasingly replacing traditional methods. With the day's bread having been made and baked in the morning, the meal is complete. Fresh fruit is served at the end of the meal, followed by mint tea and perhaps a simple cookie.

chicken soup
with couscous
. . . . serves 4

USE A WHOLE CHICKEN SUITABLE FOR STEWING AND CUT IT INTO QUARTERS, OR USE CHICKEN PIECES FOR CONVENIENCE. WHEN COOKED, THE CHICKEN MUST BE TENDER ENOUGH FOR THE MEAT TO BE EASILY REMOVED FROM THE BONES.

chicken	3 lb. 5 oz., quartered
olive oil	3 tablespoons
onions	2, finely chopped
ground cumin	1/2 teaspoon
paprika	1/2 teaspoon
harissa	1/2 teaspoon or to taste
	(or 1/4 teaspoon cayenne pepper)
tomatoes	2 medium
tomato paste	4 teaspoons
sugar	1 teaspoon
cinnamon stick	1
couscous	1/2 cup
Italian parsley	3 tablespoons finely chopped
cilantro	4 teaspoons finely chopped
dried mint	1 teaspoon
lemon wedges	to serve

Remove and discard the skin from the chicken. Heat the olive oil in a large saucepan or stockpot, add the chicken, and cook over high heat for 2–3 minutes, stirring often. Reduce the heat to medium, add the onion, and cook for 5 minutes or until the onion has softened. Stir in the cumin, paprika, and harissa or cayenne pepper. Add 4 cups water and bring to a boil.

Halve the tomatoes and squeeze out the seeds. Over a plate, coarsely grate the tomatoes down to the skin, discarding the skin. Add the grated tomato to the pot, along with the tomato paste, sugar, cinnamon stick, 1 teaspoon salt, and some freshly ground black pepper. Bring to a boil, reduce the heat to low, and then cover and simmer for 1 hour or until the chicken is very tender.

Remove the chicken to a dish with a slotted spoon. When it is cool enough to handle, remove the bones and tear the chicken meat into strips. Return the chicken to the pot with an additional 2 cups water and return to a boil. While it is boiling, gradually pour in the couscous, stirring constantly. Reduce the heat, stir in the parsley, cilantro, and mint, and simmer uncovered for 20 minutes. Adjust the seasoning to taste. Serve with lemon wedges and crusty bread.

Cut the tomatoes in half and squeeze out the seeds.

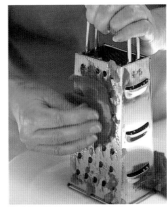

Grate the tomatoes down to the skin, then discard the skin.

kefta kabobs . . . . serves 4

THESE DELICIOUS SAUSAGE-SHAPED KABOBS ARE SOLD AS STREET FOOD IN MOROCCO, SERVED IN WEDGES OF
MOROCCAN BREAD WITH A FIERY HARISSA AND TOMATO SAUCE (PAGE 21). THEY ARE ALSO MADE INTO SMALL,
ROUND PATTIES AND CHARBROILED.

onion	1 small, roughly chopped
Italian parsley	3 tablespoons chopped
cilantro	4 teaspoons chopped
ground lamb or beef	1 lb. 2 oz.
ground cumin	1 teaspoon
paprika	1 teaspoon
cayenne pepper	1/4 teaspoon
freshly ground black pepper	1/4 teaspoon
salad greens	to serve
lemon wedges	to serve

Put the onion, parsley, and cilantro in a food processor and
process to a purée. Add the lamb or beef, cumin, paprika,
cayenne pepper, black pepper, and 1 teaspoon salt. Process to
a paste, scraping the side of the bowl occasionally.

Divide the kefta mixture into eight even portions. Moisten your
hands with water and mold each portion into a sausage shape
about 3 1/2 inches long. Place on a tray, cover with plastic wrap,
and chill for 1 hour.

Insert a flat metal skewer through the center of each kefta
sausage. Cook on a hot barbecue grill or in a charbroil pan,
turning frequently to brown evenly. Cook until they are just well
done (about 10 minutes)—they will feel firm when pressed lightly
with tongs.

Serve the keftas with salad greens and lemon wedges. Serve
with small dishes of ground cumin and salt on the side, to be
added according to individual taste.

Mold each portion of the kefta
mixture into a sausage shape.

Insert a metal skewer through
each kefta sausage.

spicy blends

Harissa (pictured below) is a hot and spicy Tunisian condiment that the Moroccans have adopted and adapted to their tastes. To make it, roughly chop 5 cups dried red chilies and soak in boiling water for 1 hour. Drain the chilies and put them in a food processor with 10 chopped garlic cloves, 4 teaspoons each of mint, ground coriander, and ground cumin, 1 teaspoon ground caraway seeds, 4 teaspoons olive oil, and 1/2 teaspoon salt. Process to a purée. With the motor running, gradually add another 1/2 cup olive oil, scraping the side of the bowl when necessary. Spoon the thick paste into a 2 1/2-cup sterilized jar. Cover the top of the harissa with a thin layer of olive oil and seal the jar. Store in the refrigerator for up to six months. Harissa is also available at gourmet food stores and Middle Eastern markets. Use it with caution, as it is very hot.

Chermoula is a marinade and sauce indispensable for cooking fish, and it can also serve as a marinade for poultry and lamb. It is an inspired blend of ingredients—cilantro, Italian parsley, garlic, onion, cumin, ground coriander, saffron, paprika, and cayenne pepper. There are many versions of this typically Moroccan marinade, with the ingredients varying depending on the cook or the food it is to be served with. Preserved lemon rind, lemon juice, or vinegar are sometimes added. Olive oil is essential.

spiced grilled chicken .... serves 4

THE MOROCCAN SPICES AND SUGAR-DIPPED, GRILLED LEMON QUARTERS ADD AN EXOTIC TOUCH TO BARBECUED
CHICKEN. WARM SQUASH SALAD WITH PRESERVED LEMON (PAGE 86) GOES WELL AS AN ACCOMPANIMENT AND CAN
BE COOKED ON THE BARBECUE ALONGSIDE THE CHICKEN.

chickens	2 x 1 lb. 10 oz.
saffron threads	a pinch
coarse salt	1 teaspoon
garlic	2 cloves, chopped
paprika	1 1/2 teaspoons
cayenne pepper	1/4 teaspoon
ground cumin	2 teaspoons
freshly ground black pepper	1/2 teaspoon
lemon juice	4 teaspoons
olive oil	4 teaspoons
lemons	2
confectioners' sugar	3 tablespoons
watercress	to serve

To prepare the chickens, cut them on each side of the backbone using poultry shears or kitchen scissors. Rinse the chickens and dry with paper towels. Open out on a board, skin side up, and press down with the heel of your hand on the top of each breast to break the breastbone and flatten it. Cut deep slashes diagonally in each breast and on the legs. Push four long metal skewers from the tip of each breast through to the underside of the legs, which should be spread outward so that the thickness of the chicken is as even as possible.

Put the saffron in a mortar with the salt and pound with a pestle to pulverize the threads. Add the garlic and pound to a paste. Work in the paprika, cayenne pepper, cumin, black pepper, lemon juice, and olive oil. Rub the spice mix into the chickens, rubbing it into the slashes. Cover and marinate in the refrigerator for at least 2 hours or overnight. Bring the chickens to room temperature 1 hour before cooking.

Prepare a charcoal fire or preheat the barbecue and place the chickens on the grill, skin side up. Cook over medium heat for 20 minutes, continually turning the chicken as it cooks and brushing with any remaining marinade. The chicken is cooked if the juices run clear when the thigh is pierced with a knife. Cooking time can be shortened on a barbecue if a roasting pan is inverted over the chickens to act as a mini oven—reduce the heat to low to prevent burning. Transfer the chickens to a platter, remove the skewers, cover with a foil tent, and set aside for 5 minutes before cutting in half to serve.

Cut the lemons in half horizontally, remove any seeds, and then cut again into quarters. Sift the confectioners' sugar onto a large plate. Dip the cut surfaces of the lemon quarters in the sugar and place on the barbecue hot plate. Cook briefly on the cut surfaces until golden and caramelized. Serve the chickens with the lemon wedges and watercress.

Press down on each chicken
breast to flatten it.

Push skewers from the breast to
the underside of the legs.

steamed lamb with cumin..serves 4

THIS IS A DISH OF SIMPLE BUT DELICIOUS FLAVORS. WHEN SERVED AS PART OF A MOROCCAN MEAL, MORSELS OF LAMB ARE GENTLY PULLED FROM THE BONE WITH THE FINGERS. HOWEVER, THE LAMB CAN BE SLICED AND SERVED WITH BEET AND CUMIN SALAD (PAGE 41) AND TINY BOILED POTATOES.

lamb shoulder on the bone	2 lb. 12 oz.
ground cumin	1½ teaspoons, plus extra to serve
coarse salt	1 teaspoon, plus extra to serve
freshly ground black pepper	½ teaspoon
ground saffron threads	a pinch
garlic	6 cloves, bruised
parsley	10–12 stalks
olive oil	4 teaspoons

Trim the excess fat from the whole shoulder of lamb if necessary. Wipe the meat with damp paper towels and then cut small incisions into the meat on each side.

Combine the cumin, salt, black pepper, and saffron and rub the mixture into the lamb, pushing it into the incisions. Cover and leave for 30 minutes for the flavors to penetrate. Place the lamb fat side up on a piece of muslin, top with half the garlic cloves, and tie the muslin over the top.

Fill a large saucepan into which a steamer will fit, or the base of a couscoussier, three-quarters full with water. If using a saucepan and steamer, check that the base of the steamer is at least 1¼ inches above the surface of the water. Cover the pan and bring to a boil. Line the base of the steamer with the parsley stalks and the remaining garlic cloves. Place the lamb on top, folding strips of foil around the rim of the steamer. Cover firmly to contain the steam. Keeping the heat just high enough to maintain a boil, steam the lamb for 2–2½ hours—do not lift the lid for the first 1½ hours of cooking. The lamb should easily pull away from the bone when cooked. Lift the lamb from the steamer and remove the muslin.

Heat the olive oil in a large frying pan and quickly brown the lamb on each side for a more attractive presentation. Serve with small dishes of coarse salt and ground cumin on the side, if desired.

Rub the spice mixture into the lamb, pushing it into the incisions.

Wrap a piece of muslin around the lamb and tie it together.

three ways with chermoula

THIS HERB AND SPICE MIX IS A MOROCCAN SPECIALTY PARTICULARLY SUITED TO SEAFOOD. THE SPICY SHRIMP RECIPE EMPHASIZES A VERSION OF CHERMOULA WITH SPICES, WHILE THE OTHER RECIPES FEATURE HERBS. THE CHERMOULA CAN BE STORED IN A SEALED JAR IN THE REFRIGERATOR FOR UP TO THREE DAYS. USE IT AS A MARINADE AND BASTE FOR BARBECUED OR CHARBROILED FISH, CALAMARI, OR BABY OCTOPUS, BUT ONLY MARINATE FISH FOR 5 MINUTES, AS THE LEMON JUICE COULD "COOK" IT.

shrimp in chermoula

Peel 2 lb. 4 oz. raw large shrimp, leaving the tails intact. To devein the shrimp, cut a slit down the back and remove any visible vein. Place the shrimp in a colander and rinse under cold running water. Shake the colander to remove any excess water, sprinkle the shrimp with 1/2 teaspoon salt, toss through, and set aside. To make the chermoula, remove the pulp from 1/2 preserved lemon, rinse the rind, and pat dry. Roughly chop and place in a food processor, along with 2 roughly chopped garlic cloves, 1/4 cup each of chopped Italian parsley and chopped cilantro, 3 tablespoons lemon juice, 1/4 teaspoon ground saffron threads if desired, 1/2 teaspoon each of paprika and ground cumin, and 1/8–1/4 teaspoon cayenne pepper to taste. Process to a coarse paste, gradually adding 1/4 cup olive oil while processing. Heat 3 tablespoons olive oil in a large frying pan over medium to high heat, then add the shrimp and cook, stirring often until they begin to turn pink. Reduce the heat to medium, add the chermoula, and continue to cook, stirring often, for 3 minutes or until the shrimp are firm. Serve hot with lemon wedges and saffron rice (page 135). Serves 4.

spicy shrimp

Prepare, rinse, and drain 13 oz. raw medium shrimp as described above. Pour 1/4 cup olive oil into a large frying pan and place over medium heat. Stir in 1/2 teaspoon ground cumin, 1/2 teaspoon cumin seeds, 1 teaspoon ground ginger, and 2 teaspoons chopped red chili. Cook until fragrant and the cumin seeds start to pop. Then add 3 finely chopped garlic cloves, 1/2 teaspoon ground turmeric, and 1 teaspoon paprika. Cook, stirring for a few seconds, then add the shrimp. Increase the heat a little and fry the shrimp, tossing frequently, for 3–4 minutes until they firm up and turn pink. Stir in 3 tablespoons finely chopped cilantro and 1/4 cup water, bring to a simmer, and remove from the heat. Serve immediately with lemon wedges. Serves 4 as an appetizer.

tuna skewers with chermoula

Soak eight bamboo skewers in water for 2 hours or use metal skewers. Cut 1 lb. 12 oz. tuna steaks into 1 1/4-inch cubes. Put the tuna in a shallow, nonmetallic dish. Combine 3 tablespoons olive oil, 1/2 teaspoon ground cumin, and 2 teaspoons finely grated lemon zest. Pour this mixture over the tuna. Toss to coat, then cover and chill for 10 minutes. To make the chermoula, cook 1/2 teaspoon ground coriander, 1 1/2 teaspoons each of ground cumin and paprika, and a pinch of cayenne pepper in a frying pan over medium heat until fragrant. Tip into a bowl, add 3 crushed garlic cloves, 1/4 cup each of chopped Italian parsley and chopped cilantro leaves, and 1/4 cup each of lemon juice and olive oil, and stir through. Thread the tuna onto the skewers. Lightly oil a charbroil pan or barbecue grill and cook the skewers for 1 minute on each side for rare, 2 minutes for medium, or until cooked to taste. Serve drizzled with the chermoula. Serves 4.

fish soup .... serves 6

WITH SUCH A WIDE VARIETY OF FISH AVAILABLE, IT IS SURPRISING THAT THERE ARE SO FEW FISH SOUP RECIPES IN MOROCCAN COOKING. THIS SOUP IS TYPICAL OF THE CUISINE IN TETUÁN, IN THE COUNTRY'S NORTH, WHERE SPANISH INFLUENCES STILL PREVAIL.

red bell peppers	2
long red chili	1
extra-virgin olive oil	3 tablespoons
onion	1, finely chopped
tomato paste	4 teaspoons
harissa	2–3 teaspoons, to taste
garlic	4 cloves, finely chopped
ground cumin	2 teaspoons
fish stock	3 cups
crushed tomatoes	14-oz. can
firm white fish, such as	
blue-eye cod or ling	1 lb. 10 oz., cut into 3/4-inch cubes
bay leaves	2
cilantro	3 tablespoons chopped

Cut the bell peppers into quarters and remove the membrane and seeds. Cut the chili in half and remove the seeds. Place the bell pepper and chili skin side up under a hot broiler and broil until the skins blacken. Remove and place in a plastic bag, tucking the end of the bag underneath to steam the peppers until cool enough to handle. Remove the skin, cut the flesh into thin strips, and set aside.

Heat the oil in a large saucepan and cook the onions for 5 minutes or until softened. Stir in the tomato paste, harissa, garlic, cumin, and 1/2 cup water. Add the stock, tomatoes, and 2 cups water. Bring to a boil, then reduce the heat and add the fish and bay leaves. Simmer for 7–8 minutes.

Remove the fish and discard the bay leaves. When the soup has cooled slightly, add half the cilantro and purée until smooth. Season to taste. Return the soup to the pan, add the fish, bell pepper, and chili, and simmer gently for 5 minutes. Garnish with the remaining cilantro and serve hot with crusty bread.

Used from antiquity in the Middle East, cumin was introduced into Morocco by the Arabs and has become one of the most popular spices, used in fish and chicken tagines and soups, and mixed with salt and sprinkled on kabobs and hard-boiled eggs. It is essential for *mechoui* (slow-roasted lamb). Many Moroccan cooks prefer to freshly pound cumin seeds to attain maximum flavor. A darker cumin—greenish-brown in color—is the one to choose, as lighter cumin could be mixed with ground coriander seeds. It should have an oily feel between the fingers with a warm and sweet, yet pungent and earthy, aroma.

saffron fish balls
in tomato sauce .... serves 4

THIS RECIPE WAS DEVISED BY MOROCCAN JEWS, WHO WERE ALSO THE PRINCIPAL GATHERERS OF THE SAFFRON CROCUS WHEN IT WAS INTRODUCED FROM MOORISH SPAIN. IT IS BASED ON THEIR TRADITIONAL RECIPE FOR FISH BALLS, BUT WITH DISTINCTIVE MOROCCAN FLAVORS. ANY WHITE FISH FILLETS CAN BE USED.

boneless white fish fillets	1 lb. 2 oz.
egg	1
scallions	2, chopped
Italian parsley	4 teaspoons chopped
cilantro	4 teaspoons chopped
fresh breadcrumbs	2/3 cup
ground saffron threads	1/8 teaspoon

tomato sauce

tomatoes	4 medium
onion	1, coarsely grated
olive oil	1/4 cup
garlic	2 cloves, finely chopped
paprika	1 teaspoon
harissa	1/2 teaspoon or to taste
	(or 1/4 teaspoon cayenne pepper)
ground cumin	1/2 teaspoon
sugar	1 teaspoon

Cut the fish fillets into rough pieces and put in a food processor, along with the egg, scallion, parsley, cilantro, and breadcrumbs. Mix the saffron with 4 teaspoons warm water and add to the other ingredients with 3/4 teaspoon salt and some freshly ground black pepper. Process to a thick paste, scraping down the side of the bowl occasionally.

With moistened hands, shape the fish mixture into balls the size of walnuts. Put on a tray, cover, and set aside in the refrigerator.

To make the tomato sauce, first peel the tomatoes by scoring a cross in the base of each one using a knife. Put them in a bowl of boiling water for 20 seconds, then plunge them into a bowl of cold water to cool. Remove from the water and peel the skin away from the cross—it should slip off easily. Halve the tomatoes and squeeze out the seeds. Chop the tomatoes and set aside.

Put the onion and olive oil in a saucepan and cook over medium heat for 5 minutes. Add the garlic, paprika, harissa or cayenne pepper, and cumin. Stir for a few seconds, then add the tomato, sugar, 1 cup water, salt, and freshly ground black pepper to taste. Bring to a boil, cover, and simmer for 15 minutes.

Add the fish balls to the tomato sauce, shaking the pan occasionally as they are added so that they settle into the sauce. Return to a gentle boil over medium heat, then cover and reduce to low heat. Simmer for 20 minutes. Serve the fish balls hot with crusty bread.

Shape the fish mixture into balls the size of walnuts.

Peel the tomato skin away from the cross.

three ways with chickpeas

THE CHICKPEA HAS BEEN USED AS A FOOD IN THE MEDITERRANEAN REGION SINCE ANCIENT TIMES. IN MOROCCO, WHERE OFTEN ONLY A SMALL AMOUNT OF MEAT AND CHICKEN IS USED IN A DISH, CHICKPEAS ADD SUBSTANCE AND NUTRITIONAL VALUE. MOROCCAN COOKS USUALLY SKIN THE CHICKPEAS (SEE PAGE 110) WHEN ADDING THEM TO TAGINES, BUT NOT FOR SOUPS OR FOR STREET FOOD AS IN THE RECIPE FOR HOT CHICKPEAS. THESE CHICKPEAS ARE DRAINED OF EXCESS LIQUID AFTER COOKING AND SERVED IN PAPER CONES.

hot chickpeas

Use either 1 cup dried chickpeas or two 15-oz. cans of chickpeas. To cook dried chickpeas, soak them overnight in three times their volume of cold water. Drain, place in a saucepan with fresh water to cover, and simmer gently for 1 hour or until tender, adding salt to taste near the end of cooking. Drain, reserving 1 cup of the cooking liquid. If using canned chickpeas, drain them, reserving 1 cup of the liquid. Warm 3 tablespoons olive oil in a saucepan over medium heat. Add 1 finely chopped onion and cook until lightly golden, then add 1 chopped small green bell pepper, 1 teaspoon ground cumin, and 3 tablespoons finely chopped cilantro and cook for a few seconds. Add the chickpeas and their liquid, and freshly ground black pepper to taste. Cover and bring to a simmer until heated through. Adjust the seasoning and serve hot in small bowls with bread. Serves 4–6.

tagine of chickpeas

Put $1/4$ cup olive oil and 1 chopped onion in a large saucepan and cook over medium heat for 7–8 minutes or until softened. Stir in 1 finely chopped garlic clove, 1 teaspoon harissa (or $1/4$ teaspoon cayenne pepper) to taste, $1/2$ teaspoon paprika, $1/4$ teaspoon ground ginger, $1/2$ teaspoon ground turmeric, 1 teaspoon ground cumin, and 1 teaspoon ground cinnamon. Cook gently for 2 minutes. Add a 14-oz. can chopped tomatoes and 1 teaspoon sugar. Season to taste. Cover and simmer for 20 minutes. Meanwhile, drain two 15-oz. cans chickpeas and put them in a large bowl with enough cold water to cover well. Lift up handfuls of chickpeas and rub them between your hands to loosen the skins. Run more water into the bowl and stir well. Let the skins float to the top and skim them off. Repeat until all the skins have been removed. Drain the chickpeas again and stir them into the tomato mixture. Cover and simmer for 20–25 minutes, adding a little more water if necessary. Stir through $1/4$ cup chopped Italian parsley and 3 tablespoons chopped cilantro. Season to taste. Serve with crusty bread or with couscous. Serves 4.

chickpea and saffron soup

Put 3 tablespoons olive oil and 1 finely chopped onion in a large saucepan. Cook over low heat for 5 minutes to soften. Add 1 crushed garlic clove and $1/4$ teaspoon each of ground ginger, turmeric, and pepper. Cook for a few seconds. Stir in 4 cups chicken or vegetable stock, $1/4$ teaspoon ground saffron threads, 1 tablespoon tomato paste, and $1/4$ cup chopped Italian parsley. Drain and rinse a 15-oz. can chickpeas and add to the pan. Bring to a boil, cover, and simmer gently for 40 minutes. Season to taste and serve hot. Serves 4.

spiced lentil and squash tagine

THERE ARE FEW TRULY VEGETARIAN RECIPES IN MOROCCAN COOKING, BUT THIS IS ONE OF THEM—AND A DELICIOUS AND NUTRITIOUS ONE AT THAT. THE EARTHY FLAVOR OF LENTILS COMBINES WITH THE SWEETNESS OF THE SQUASH, THE FLAVORS MELDING WITH TRADITIONAL HERBS AND SPICES.

brown lentils	1 1/2 cups
tomatoes	2 medium
butternut squash	1 (1–1 1/2 lb.)
olive oil	1/4 cup
onion	1, finely chopped
garlic	3 cloves, finely chopped
ground cumin	1/2 teaspoon
ground turmeric	1/2 teaspoon
cayenne pepper	1/8 teaspoon (or 1 teaspoon harissa, to taste)
paprika	1 teaspoon
tomato paste	1 tablespoon
sugar	1/2 teaspoon
Italian parsley	4 teaspoons finely chopped
cilantro	3 tablespoons chopped

Rinse the lentils in a sieve. Tip into a saucepan and add 4 cups cold water. Bring to a boil, skim the surface if necessary, then cover and simmer over low heat for 20 minutes.

Meanwhile, halve the tomatoes and squeeze out the seeds. In a bowl, coarsely grate the tomatoes down to the skin, discarding the skins. Set the tomato aside. Peel and seed the squash and cut into 1 1/4-inch cubes. Set aside.

Heat the oil in a large saucepan, add the onion, and cook over low heat until softened. Add the garlic, cook for a few seconds, and then stir in the cumin, turmeric, and cayenne pepper or harissa. Cook for 30 seconds, then add the grated tomatoes, paprika, tomato paste, sugar, half the parsley and cilantro, 1 teaspoon salt, and freshly ground black pepper to taste. Add the drained lentils and chopped squash, stir well, and then cover and simmer for 20 minutes or until the squash and lentils are tender. Adjust the seasoning and sprinkle with the remaining parsley and cilantro. Serve hot or warm with crusty bread.

There is considerable confusion in some quarters as to what constitutes a pumpkin. The large, orange pumpkin with fibrous flesh is often looked upon with disdain, but can be good for soups and purées. If only these are available, choose small specimens. However, the pumpkins known as winter squash are an entirely different matter. Choose those that have a firm orange flesh and are of a reasonable size. Butternut squash is a variety that is widely available, but experiment with what is available in your area.

chicken k'dra with chickpeas..................................serves 4

A K'DRA IS A BERBER METHOD OF COOKING CHICKEN, CHARACTERIZED BY THE LARGE AMOUNT OF HERBED SMEN AND ONIONS USED, AS WELL AS CHICKPEAS AND SAFFRON. THE AMOUNT OF SMEN (CLARIFIED BUTTER) IN THE FOLLOWING RECIPE HAS BEEN REDUCED. BUTTER CAN BE USED INSTEAD OF SMEN.

smen or butter	4 tablespoons
onions	3, thinly sliced
ground ginger	1/2 teaspoon
freshly ground black pepper	1/2 teaspoon
chicken	3 lb. 5 oz., quartered
ground saffron threads	1/4 teaspoon
cinnamon stick	1
chickpeas	2 x 15 oz. cans
Italian parsley	1/4 cup finely chopped, plus extra to serve
lemon wedges	to serve

Melt the smen or butter in a large saucepan. Add a third of the onion and cook over medium heat for 5 minutes or until softened. Add the ginger, pepper, and chicken pieces and cook without browning for 2–3 minutes, turning the chicken occasionally. Add the remaining onion, about 1 1/4 cups water, the saffron, cinnamon stick, and 1 teaspoon salt. Bring to a slow boil, reduce to low heat, and then cover and simmer gently for 45 minutes.

Meanwhile, drain the chickpeas and place them in a large bowl with cold water to cover. Lift up handfuls of chickpeas and rub them between your hands to loosen the skins, dropping them back into the bowl. Run more water into the bowl and stir well. Let the skins float to the top, then skim them off. Repeat until all the skins have been removed. Add the chickpeas to the chicken, along with the chopped parsley. Stir gently, then cover and simmer for 15 minutes or until the chicken is tender.

Tilt the saucepan, spoon off some of the fat from the surface, and put it into a frying pan. Lift out the chicken pieces, allowing the sauce to drain back into the saucepan. Heat the fat in the frying pan and brown the chicken pieces quickly over high heat. Meanwhile, boil the sauce to reduce it a little.

Serve the chicken with the chickpeas and the sauce spooned on top. Sprinkle with the extra parsley and serve with lemon wedges and crusty bread.

Cover the drained chickpeas with cold water.

Skim off the chickpea skins as they float to the top.

lamb tagine with sweet tomato jam

.... serves 4–6

TOMATO JAM IS SERVED AS AN APPETIZER—LIKE A DIP—BUT THE SAME INGREDIENTS COMBINE WITH LAMB TO GIVE A BEAUTIFULLY FLAVORED TAGINE, REDOLENT WITH CINNAMON AND HONEY. IT IS PREFERABLE TO USE FRESH TOMATOES RATHER THAN CANNED.

olive oil	3 tablespoons
lamb shoulder or leg steaks	2 lb. 4 oz., trimmed and cut into 1¼-inch-thick pieces
onions	2, coarsely grated
ripe tomatoes	12 medium, halved horizontally
garlic	2 cloves, finely chopped
ground ginger	1 teaspoon
freshly ground black pepper	¼ teaspoon
cinnamon stick	1
tomato paste	¼ cup
ground saffron threads	⅛ teaspoon, optional
butter	2 tablespoons
blanched almonds	¼ cup
honey	3 tablespoons
ground cinnamon	1½ teaspoons

Heat half the oil in a heavy-based saucepan over high heat and brown the lamb in batches. Remove and set aside. Reduce the heat to low. Add the remaining oil and the onion and cook gently, stirring occasionally for 10 minutes or until the onion is softened.

Meanwhile, squeeze out the tomato seeds. Coarsely grate the tomatoes down to the skin, discarding the skin. Stir the garlic, ginger, pepper, and cinnamon into the pan and cook for 1 minute. Add the tomato paste and saffron, if using, and cook for 1 minute. Return the lamb to the pan, stir in the grated tomato, and season. Cover and simmer gently for 1¼ hours. Simmer partly covered for 15 minutes, stirring occasionally, then uncover and simmer for 25 minutes or until the sauce has thickened and has an almost jamlike consistency with the oil beginning to separate.

Meanwhile, melt the butter in a small frying pan, add the almonds, and cook over medium heat, stirring occasionally until golden. Stir the honey and ground cinnamon into the tagine and simmer for 2 minutes. Serve with couscous, sprinkled with the almonds.

The finely shaved bark of the cinnamon tree, *Cinnamomum zeylanicum,* is interleaved and rolled to form sticks or quills about 3¼ inches long. Cassia is from another species of cinnamon tree, *Cinnamomum cassia.* It has a highly perfumed aroma and is bittersweet. It is also available in sticks made of shaved bark, with "leaves" visibly thicker than those in cinnamon sticks. It is more reddish-brown than cinnamon but can be used in place of cinnamon sticks; in fact it is often sold as such. Ground cinnamon often includes cassia (if it is brownish-red, it probably contains cassia). Both these spices, ground and in sticks, are used in savory and sweet dishes and pastries.

three ways with prunes

THE PRUNE IS THE DRIED VERSION OF VARIOUS SPECIES OF THE DAMASCENE (DAMSON) PLUM. IT IS OFTEN A SUBSTITUTE FOR DATES IN MEAT AND FRUIT TAGINES BUT IS INCREASINGLY USED IN ITS OWN RIGHT—AN INTENSELY FLAVORED SWEET AND SOUR FRUIT THAT MARRIES WELL WITH SPICES. TODAY'S PRUNES DO NOT NEED SOAKING— THEY ARE MOIST AND SUCCULENT AND ADD A WONDERFUL FLAVOR TO MOROCCAN DISHES. WHILE IT IS AN EASY (THOUGH SOMEWHAT STICKY) TASK TO REMOVE THE PITS, PITTED PRUNES ARE READILY AVAILABLE.

lamb shank and prune tagine

You will need 4 frenched lamb shanks. (Frenched lamb shanks are trimmed of excess fat with the knuckle end of the bone sawn off.) If unavailable, use whole shanks and ask the butcher to saw them in half for you. Place a heavy-based saucepan over high heat, add 4 teaspoons oil, 2 tablespoons butter, and the lamb shanks. Brown the shanks on all sides and place on a plate. Reduce the heat to medium, add 1 chopped onion, and cook gently for 5 minutes to soften. Add 1 1/2 cups water, 1/4 teaspoon ground saffron threads, 1/2 teaspoon ground ginger, 2 cinnamon sticks, and 4 cilantro sprigs tied in a bunch. Season to taste. Stir well and return the lamb shanks to the pan. Cover and simmer over low heat for 1 hour. Cut the zest of 1/2 lemon into wide strips. Add to the pan and cook for an additional 30 minutes. Add 1 1/3 cups pitted prunes and 3 tablespoons honey. Cover and simmer for an additional 30 minutes until the lamb is very tender. Remove and discard the cilantro sprigs. Serve hot, sprinkled with 4 teaspoons roasted sesame seeds. Serves 4.

spiced chicken with prunes

Melt 2 tablespoons butter in a covered frying pan. Add 1 1/2 teaspoons *ras el hanout* and stir over low heat for 30 seconds. Increase the heat to medium, add 4 x 6 oz. chicken breast fillets, and cook for 1 minute on each side without allowing the spices to burn. Remove the chicken from the pan. Add 1 sliced onion to the pan and cook over medium heat for 5 minutes. Pour in 1 cup chicken stock and add 2/3 cup pitted prunes and 1 tablespoon each of honey, lemon juice, and rosewater. Cover and simmer over low heat for 10 minutes. Return the chicken to the pan, cover, and simmer gently for 15 minutes. Slice the chicken breasts diagonally and serve with the prune sauce and steamed couscous (page 140). Serves 4.

roast vegetables with prunes

Pour 1/4 cup olive oil into a 12 x 16 x 2 1/2-inch ovenproof dish and add 2 peeled and quartered red onions, 3 bruised unpeeled garlic cloves, and 2 sliced carrots. Toss well. Bake in a preheated 400°F oven for 15 minutes. Peel and cut 1 lb. firm squash and 1 large orange sweet potato into large cubes. Add to the dish, along with 1 1/2 teaspoons *ras el hanout* and 1 seeded and sliced red chili. Season and toss well. Bake for an additional 30 minutes. Stir in 1 1/2 cups light chicken or vegetable stock, 1 cup pitted prunes, and 4 teaspoons honey and return to the oven for an additional 30 minutes. Serve with steamed couscous (page 140) or as a vegetable accompaniment. Serves 4.

beef tagine with sweet potatoes

USE THE ORANGE-FLESHED SWEET POTATO, AS IT IS MEALY AND SWEET AND KEEPS ITS SHAPE WHEN COOKED. THE TAGINE IS FINISHED AND BROWNED IN THE OVEN; IN TRADITIONAL MOROCCAN COOKING, IT WOULD BE COVERED WITH A METAL LID WITH GLOWING CHARCOAL PLACED ON TOP—VERY EFFECTIVE.

blade or chuck steak	2 lb. 4 oz.
olive oil	1/4 cup
onion	1, finely chopped
cayenne pepper	1/2 teaspoon
ground cumin	1/2 teaspoon
ground turmeric	1 teaspoon
ground ginger	1/2 teaspoon
paprika	2 teaspoons
Italian parsley	3 tablespoons chopped
cilantro	3 tablespoons chopped
tomatoes	2 medium
orange sweet potato	1 large

Trim the steak of any fat and cut into 1-inch pieces. Heat half the oil in a saucepan and brown the beef in batches over high heat, adding a little more oil as needed. Set aside in a dish.

Reduce the heat to low, add the onion and the remaining oil to the pan, and gently cook for 10 minutes or until the onion is softened. Add the cayenne pepper, cumin, turmeric, ginger, and paprika, cook for a few seconds, and then add 1 teaspoon salt and a good grinding of black pepper. Return the beef to the pan and add the parsley, cilantro, and 1 cup water. Cover and simmer over low heat for 1 1/2 hours or until the meat is almost tender.

Peel the tomatoes. To do this, score a cross in the base of each one using a knife. Put the tomatoes in a bowl of boiling water for 20 seconds, then plunge them into a bowl of cold water to cool. Remove from the water and peel the skin away from the cross—it should slip off easily. Slice the tomatoes. Peel the sweet potato, cut it into 3/4-inch cubes, and leave in cold water until required, as this will prevent it from discoloring. Preheat the oven to 350°F.

Transfer the meat and its sauce to an ovenproof serving dish (the base of a tagine would be ideal). Drain the sweet potato and spread it over the top of the beef. Top with the tomato slices. Cover with foil (or the lid of the tagine) and bake for 40 minutes. Remove the foil, increase the oven temperature to 425°F, and move the dish to the upper oven shelf. Cook until the tomatoes and sweet potato are tender and flecked with brown. Serve from the dish.

Peel the skin from the tomatoes before slicing them.

Peel the sweet potatoes and cut them into cubes.

lamb tagine with peas and lemons

PRESERVED LEMONS ADD A WONDERFUL FLAVOR TO THIS DELICIOUS COMBINATION OF LAMB, GREEN PEAS, FRESH HERBS, AND GROUND SPICES. WHILE SHELLED FRESH GREEN PEAS ARE PREFERRED, FROZEN PEAS ALSO GIVE GOOD RESULTS.

lamb shoulder or leg	2 lb. 4 oz., boned
olive oil	3 tablespoons
onion	1, finely chopped
garlic	2 cloves, finely chopped
ground cumin	1 teaspoon
ground ginger	1/2 teaspoon
ground turmeric	1/2 teaspoon
cilantro	1/4 cup chopped
Italian parsley	1/4 cup chopped
lemon thyme	2 teaspoons chopped
preserved lemons	1 1/2
peas	1 1/2 cups
mint	2 teaspoons chopped
sugar	1/2 teaspoon

Trim the lamb and cut into 1 1/4-inch pieces. Heat the oil in a large saucepan over high heat and brown the lamb in batches, placing in a dish when cooked. Add more oil if needed.

Reduce the heat to low, add the onion, and cook for 5 minutes or until softened. Add the garlic, cumin, ginger, and turmeric and cook for a few seconds. Add 1 1/2 cups water and stir well to lift the browned juices off the base of the pan. Return the lamb to the pan with a little salt and a good grinding of black pepper. Add the cilantro, parsley, and thyme. Cover and simmer over low heat for 1 1/2 hours or until the lamb is tender.

Separate the preserved lemons into quarters and rinse well under cold running water, removing and discarding the pulp. Cut the rind into strips and add to the lamb, along with the peas, mint, and sugar. Return to a simmer, cover, and simmer for an additional 10 minutes or until the peas are cooked. Serve hot.

Essential in Moroccan cooking, cilantro, the seeds of which are known as coriander, has feathery green leaves with a somewhat pungent, lemony flavor. It is native to the Middle East and southern Europe, and has been used as a culinary herb for millennia. The plant could have been introduced into the region from antiquity, as it was favored by the Greeks and Romans. The dried seeds are ground and used as a spice, with a combined lemon zest and sage flavor. Dried coriander complements cumin but is not used as frequently as cumin; however, it is one of the spices used in *ras el hanout* (page 113).

kefta tagine .... serves 4

FOR COMMUNAL EATING IN THE MOROCCAN MANNER, THIS DISH IS SERVED AT THE TABLE IN THE DISH IN WHICH IT IS COOKED. WITH THE AID OF BREAD, DINERS MANAGE TO GET THEIR FAIR PORTION OF THE EGG. BREAD IS ALSO A MUST FOR MOPPING UP THE FULL-FLAVORED SAUCE.

ground lamb	1 lb. 9 oz.
onion	1 small, finely chopped
garlic	2 cloves, finely chopped
Italian parsley	3 tablespoons finely chopped
cilantro	3 tablespoons finely chopped leaves
cayenne pepper	1/2 teaspoon
ground ginger	1/2 teaspoon
ground cumin	1 teaspoon
paprika	1 teaspoon
oil	3 tablespoons

sauce

olive oil	3 tablespoons
onion	1, finely chopped
garlic	2 cloves, finely chopped
ground cumin	2 teaspoons
ground cinnamon	1/2 teaspoon
paprika	1 teaspoon
chopped tomatoes	1 lb. 12 oz. can
harissa	2 teaspoons or to taste
cilantro	1/3 cup chopped
eggs	4

Put the lamb, onion, garlic, herbs, and spices in a bowl and mix well. Season with salt and freshly ground black pepper. Roll 4 teaspoons of the mixture into a ball. Repeat with the remaining lamb mixture.

Heat the oil in a large covered frying pan over medium to high heat. Add the meatballs in batches. Cook, turning occasionally, for 8–10 minutes or until browned all over. Remove the meatballs and set aside in a bowl. Wipe the frying pan with paper towels.

To make the sauce, heat the olive oil in the frying pan, add the onion, and cook over medium heat for 5 minutes or until the onion is soft. Add the garlic, cumin, cinnamon, and paprika and cook for 1 minute or until fragrant. Stir in the tomato and harissa and bring to a boil. Reduce the heat and simmer for 20 minutes.

Add the meatballs, cover, and simmer for 10 minutes or until cooked. Stir in the cilantro, then carefully break the eggs into the simmering tagine and cook until just set. (Alternatively, transfer the meatballs and sauce to a large, shallow, ovenproof serving dish. Add the eggs and cook in a preheated 400°F oven for 5–8 minutes or until the eggs are set.) Season and serve with crusty bread to mop up the juices.

Roll 4 teaspoons of the lamb mixture into a ball.

Carefully break 4 eggs into the simmering tagine.

three ways with squash

THE MOROCCAN PUMPKIN, *KAR'A LHAMRA*, IS ROUND AND ORANGE-SKINNED, AND IS FIRMER AND SWEETER THAN THE HALLOWEEN TYPE. THE BUTTERNUT SQUASH IS ALSO USED; OTHER WINTER SQUASH IS SUITABLE AS LONG AS IT IS HEAVY FOR ITS SIZE, THE FLESH IS FIRM, SWEET, AND ORANGE-COLORED, AND IT HAS A HARD SKIN THAT HAS TO BE PEELED. SQUASH IS USED FOR VEGETABLE TAGINES, AS A WARM SALAD OR APPETIZER TO ACCOMPANY MAIN MEALS, AND OFTEN IN STEWS FOR SERVING WITH COUSCOUS.

squash and sweet potato tagine

Peel and cube 1/2 small butternut squash and 1 large orange sweet potato. Melt 4 tablespoons butter in a large saucepan over low heat. Add 1 finely chopped large onion and cook gently, stirring occasionally until softened. Add 2 finely chopped garlic cloves, 1 teaspoon each of ground ginger and turmeric, 1 cinnamon stick, and a pinch of cayenne pepper. Stir over low heat for 1–2 minutes. Pour in 2 cups vegetable or chicken stock, add 1/8 teaspoon ground saffron threads, and then increase the heat to medium and bring to a boil. Add the squash, sweet potato, 1/2 cup raisins, and 4 teaspoons honey. Season with salt and freshly ground black pepper. Cover and simmer for an additional 15 minutes or until the vegetables are tender. Remove the cinnamon stick, transfer the tagine to a bowl, and sprinkle with cilantro leaves. Serve with couscous or as an accompaniment. Serves 4–6.

warm squash salad with preserved lemon

Peel and remove the seeds from 1 small butternut squash. Cut the squash into 3/4-inch cubes. Remove the pulp from 1 preserved lemon and rinse and dice the rind. Heat 1/4 cup olive oil in a large covered frying pan. Add 1 grated onion and cook over medium heat for 3 minutes. Stir in 1/2 teaspoon each of ground ginger and cumin and 1 teaspoon paprika and cook for an additional 30 seconds. Add the squash, 3 tablespoons each of chopped Italian parsley and cilantro, 4 teaspoons lemon juice, the preserved lemon rind, and 1/2 cup water. Season to taste, cover, and simmer over low heat for 20 minutes or until tender, tossing occasionally with a spatula and adding a little more water if necessary. Serve warm as an appetizer or hot as a vegetable accompaniment. Serves 4.

roast squash with orange and spices

Peel and remove the seeds from 1 small butternut squash. Cut the squash into 3/4-inch cubes. Put the squash in a roasting pan with 3 tablespoons oil and toss to coat. Combine the grated zest and juice of 1 orange and pour over the squash. Sprinkle with 1 1/2 teaspoons *ras el hanout*, season, and drizzle with 1 tablespoon honey. Roast in a preheated 400°F oven for 45 minutes, tossing occasionally with a spatula. Serve hot or warm as an appetizer or vegetable accompaniment. Serves 4.

meatball tagine with herbs and lemon . . . . serves 4

THE MEATBALLS IN THIS DISH DO NOT NEED TO BE BROWNED. SPICES, COMBINED WITH FRESH ITALIAN PARSLEY AND CILANTRO AND THE HEAT OF A FRESH CHILI, ARE USED WITH LEMON TO MAKE A DELICIOUS SAUCE IN WHICH TO COOK THEM.

onion	1/2, roughly chopped
Italian parsley	3 tablespoons roughly chopped
white bread	2 slices, crusts removed
egg	1
ground lamb or beef	1 lb. 2 oz.
ground cumin	1/2 teaspoon
paprika	1/2 teaspoon
freshly ground black pepper	1/2 teaspoon

herb and lemon sauce

butter or oil	4 teaspoons
onion	1/2, finely chopped
paprika	1/2 teaspoon
ground turmeric	1/2 teaspoon
ground cumin	1/4 teaspoon
red chili	1, seeded and sliced
	(or 1/4 teaspoon cayenne pepper)
chicken stock	1 1/2 cups
cilantro	3 tablespoons chopped leaves
Italian parsley	3 tablespoons chopped
lemon juice	3 tablespoons
preserved lemon	1/2, optional

Put the onion and parsley in a food processor and process until finely chopped. Tear the bread into pieces, add to the onion, along with the egg, and process briefly. Add the lamb or beef, cumin, paprika, pepper, and 1 teaspoon salt and process to a thick paste, scraping down the side of the bowl occasionally. Alternatively, grate the onion, chop the parsley, crumb the bread, and add to the lamb or beef in a bowl with the egg, spices, and seasoning. Knead until the mixture is pastelike in consistency.

With moistened hands, shape the mixture into walnut-sized balls and place them on a tray. Cover and refrigerate until required.

To make the herb and lemon sauce, heat the butter or oil in a saucepan and add the onion. Cook over low heat until softened and golden. Then add the paprika, turmeric, cumin, and chili or cayenne pepper and cook for 1 minute, stirring. Add the chicken stock and cilantro and bring to a boil.

Add the meatballs to the pan, shaking so that they settle into the sauce. Cover and simmer for 45 minutes. Add most of the parsley and the lemon juice and season if necessary. Return to a boil and simmer for 2 minutes. If using preserved lemon, rinse well under running water, remove and discard the pulp, and cut the rind into strips. Add to the meatballs. Transfer to a tagine or bowl, sprinkle with the remaining parsley, and serve hot with crusty bread.

vegetables with lamb stuffing .... serves 4

HERE IS ONE VERSION OF MOROCCAN STUFFED VEGETABLES. MOROCCAN COOKS TAKE THE TIME TO HOLLOW OUT THE ZUCCHINI BEFORE FILLING THEM, BUT IT IS ACCEPTABLE TO HALVE THEM, SCOOP OUT THE CENTERS, FILL THEM WITH THE STUFFING, AND REASSEMBLE.

zucchini	4 medium
bell peppers	2 small
tomatoes	6 medium
olive oil	3 tablespoons
onion	1, finely chopped
garlic	2 cloves, finely chopped
ground ginger	1/2 teaspoon
ground cinnamon	1/2 teaspoon
freshly ground black pepper	1/4 teaspoon
ground lamb or beef	1 lb. 2 oz.
Italian parsley	3 tablespoons chopped
cilantro	4 teaspoons chopped leaves
mint	2 teaspoons chopped
short-grain rice	1/4 cup

tomato sauce

tomato	1 large
olive oil	4 teaspoons
onion	1, coarsely grated
garlic	1 clove, finely chopped
paprika	1/2 teaspoon
ground cumin	1/4 teaspoon
tomato paste	3 tablespoons
sugar	1 teaspoon
lemon juice	4 teaspoons

Halve the zucchini lengthwise. Scoop out the centers, leaving a 1/2-inch border. Halve the bell peppers lengthwise; remove the seeds and membrane. Slice the tops from 4 tomatoes (reserve the tops), scoop out the centers, and rub the pulp through a sieve into a bowl and set aside. Peel the remaining tomatoes by scoring a cross in the base of each one using a knife. Put them in a bowl of boiling water for 20 seconds, then plunge them into a bowl of cold water to cool. Remove from the water and peel the skin away from the cross—it should slip off easily. Thinly slice the tomatoes and set aside.

Put the oil and onion in a pan and cook over medium heat for 5 minutes. Stir in the garlic, ginger, cinnamon, and pepper. Then stir in the lamb or beef. Add 1 cup water, the parsley, cilantro, mint, and 1 teaspoon salt. Bring to a boil, then cover and simmer over low heat for 20 minutes. Stir in the rice, cover, and cook for 10 minutes or until most of the liquid has been absorbed.

To make the tomato sauce, first peel the tomato (see above). Halve the tomato and squeeze out the seeds. Chop the tomato and add to the reserved tomato pulp, along with the remaining sauce ingredients and 1/2 cup water. Season to taste. Preheat the oven to 350°F.

Loosely fill the vegetables with the stuffing. Fill four zucchini halves and top each with an unfilled half, securing with wooden toothpicks. Fill the bell peppers and arrange tomato slices over the top; fill the tomatoes and replace the tops. Arrange the vegetables in an ovenproof dish. Pour in the sauce, cover with foil, and bake for 50 minutes. Remove the foil, baste the vegetables with sauce, and bake for another 10 minutes or until tender. Remove the toothpicks from the zucchini and serve.

Scoop out the centers of the zucchini, leaving a border.

Loosely fill the vegetables with the stuffing.

fish tagine with tomato and potato

WHEN COOKING FISH IN A TAGINE, MOROCCAN COOKS PREVENT IT FROM STICKING TO THE BASE OF THE TAGINE BY USING CRISSCROSSED BAMBOO CANES, PIECES OF CELERY, OR CARROT STICKS. THE POTATO SLICES USED IN THIS RECIPE SERVE THE SAME PURPOSE—AND BECOME A DELICIOUS PART OF THE DISH.

chermoula

garlic	2 cloves, roughly chopped
Italian parsley	1/4 cup chopped
cilantro	1/4 cup chopped leaves
paprika	2 teaspoons
ground cumin	2 teaspoons
cayenne pepper	1/4 teaspoon
lemon juice	4 teaspoons
olive oil	3 tablespoons

firm white fish cutlets (steaks), such as snapper, blue eye cod, hake, or sea bass	4 x 3/4 inch thick
potatoes	3 medium
tomatoes	3 medium
green bell pepper	1
tomato paste	2 tablespoons
sugar	1 teaspoon
lemon juice	4 teaspoons
olive oil	3 tablespoons
Italian parsley	4 teaspoons chopped
cilantro	4 teaspoons chopped

To make the chermoula, use a mortar and pestle to pound the garlic to a paste with 1/2 teaspoon salt. Add the parsley, cilantro, paprika, cumin, cayenne pepper, and lemon juice. Pound the mixture to a rough paste and work in the olive oil.

Rub half the chermoula on each side of the fish and place the fish in a dish, covering and setting aside for 20 minutes.

Cut the potatoes and tomatoes into 1/4-inch-thick slices. Remove the seeds and white membrane from the bell pepper and cut into strips of the same thickness. Preheat the oven to 400°F.

Brush a 12 x 16 x 2 1/2-inch ovenproof dish with oil. Place a layer of potato slices in the bottom. Put the fish on top. Toss the remaining potato slices with the remaining chermoula and arrange over the fish. Top the tagine with the tomato slices and bell pepper strips. Mix the tomato paste with 1/2 cup water and add 1/2 teaspoon salt, a good grinding of black pepper, the sugar, lemon juice, and olive oil. Pour over the fish and sprinkle with the combined parsley and cilantro.

Cover the dish with foil and bake for 40 minutes. Then remove the foil and move the dish to the upper rack. Cook for an additional 10 minutes or until the fish and potatoes are tender and the top is lightly crusted. Serve hot.

Add the herbs, spices, and lemon juice to the garlic paste.

Work the olive oil into the chermoula paste.

the souks

The *souks*, or markets, of Morocco are just one of the places from which Moroccans buy their food, but these are by far the most fascinating, especially those located within the ancient walls of the *medina*, the ancient Arab quarter. Rows of small stalls, their tables piled high with the season's produce, provide a riot of magnificent color—rich red tomatoes; a tumble of bright orange carrots; glossy green and red bell peppers; purple eggplants; red, golden, and white onions; crisp white turnips; waxy green cucumbers and zucchini; red and white radishes; and young green peas.

Men sit at their stalls, offering wild artichokes, tender wild asparagus, fragrant strawberries, or freshly laid eggs from their woven baskets or wooden crates. Nearby, a trolley might be laden with cilantro, another with fragrant mint, while the smell of freshly baked bread wafts from a cloth-covered table of wooden crates. Open-fronted shops display an array of spices, as well as a selection of olives and preserved lemons; fresh dates, figs, nuts, and raisins; chickpeas and couscous; or slabs of nougat studded with almonds.

The stalls of the meat market are jammed too. Sides of lamb hang from the roof and camel haunches are offered. Cages hold rabbits, chickens, ducks, and squabs, usually sold live, but the poultry seller will dispatch and pluck the birds on request.

Shoppers move purposefully, and male shoppers bargain for the best price. The haggling, the shouting, the braying of donkeys, the smell of kabobs cooking, the pervading aromas of spices and mint all combine to make shopping in the *souk* an unforgettable experience.

tagine of lamb, olives, and potatoes.............................serves 4–6

SAFFRON PERFUMES THE POTATOES AND GIVES THEM A GOLDEN GLOW. IF YOU CAN PURCHASE CRACKED GREEN OLIVES, SO MUCH THE BETTER: BLANCH THEM FOR 2 MINUTES ONLY, WHICH CAN READILY REMOVE THE BITTERNESS.

boneless lamb shoulder	2 lb. 4 oz., trimmed
olive oil	1/3 cup
onions	2, finely chopped
garlic	2 cloves, finely chopped
ground cumin	1 teaspoon
ground ginger	1/2 teaspoon
paprika	1/2 teaspoon
cilantro	1/4 cup chopped
Italian parsley	1/4 cup chopped
green olives	1 cup
potatoes	5 medium
ground saffron threads	1/4 teaspoon

Cut the lamb into 1 1/4-inch-thick pieces. Heat 3 tablespoons of the olive oil in a large saucepan over high heat. In batches, brown the lamb on each side, placing in a dish when done. Add a little more oil as needed.

Reduce the heat to low, add 2 tablespoons of olive oil, and cook the onion for 5 minutes or until softened. Add the garlic, cumin, and ginger and cook for a few seconds. Add 1 1/2 cups water and stir well to lift the browned juices off the base of the pan. Return the lamb to the pan, along with the paprika, 1/2 teaspoon salt, and a good grinding of black pepper. Add the cilantro and parsley. Cover and simmer over low heat for 1–1 1/4 hours.

Meanwhile, put the olives in a small saucepan, cover with water, bring to a boil, and cook for 5 minutes. Drain and repeat once more to sweeten the flavor. Add the drained olives to the lamb, cover, and cook for an additional 15–30 minutes or until the lamb is tender.

Peel the potatoes and cut them into quarters. Put in a pan, cover with lightly salted water, and add the saffron. Bring to a boil and cook for 10 minutes or until tender. Drain and toss lightly with the remaining olive oil.

Transfer the lamb and sauce to a serving dish, arrange the potatoes around the lamb, and serve.

couscous with chicken and vegetables
.... serves 4

THIS IS ONE OF THE MOST FREQUENTLY PREPARED COUSCOUS DISHES IN MOROCCAN HOUSEHOLDS ON FRIDAYS—
THE TRADITIONAL DAY FOR SERVING COUSCOUS. PRESENT IT AS DESCRIBED BELOW, OR ARRANGE THE CHICKEN
AND VEGETABLES ON A PLATTER, WITH THE COUSCOUS AND SAUCE SERVED SEPARATELY.

tomatoes	3 medium
smen or ghee	1/4 cup
chicken	3 lb. 8 oz., cut into 8 pieces
onion	1, finely chopped
ground turmeric	1/2 teaspoon
ground cumin	1/2 teaspoon
pearl or boiling onions	8, trimmed
ground saffron threads	1/4 teaspoon
cinnamon stick	1
cilantro	4 sprigs
Italian parsley	4 sprigs
carrots	3, cut into chunks
zucchini	4, cut into chunks
peas	1 1/3 cups (or very young fava beans)

spiced couscous

couscous	4–5 servings (page 140)
smen or butter	1/4 cup
chickpeas	15-oz. can, rinsed and drained
harissa	1 tablespoon or to taste

Peel the tomatoes by scoring a cross in the base of each one with a knife. Put them in a bowl of boiling water for 20 seconds, then plunge them into a bowl of cold water to cool. Remove from the water and peel the skin away from the cross— it should slip off easily. Cut the tomatoes in half and squeeze out the seeds. Chop the tomatoes and set aside.

Heat the smen or ghee in a large saucepan or the base of a large couscoussier, add the chicken, and brown briefly on each side. Reduce the heat, add the chopped onion, and cook gently until the onion has softened. Stir in the turmeric and cumin and add the onions. Pour in 3 cups water, then add the saffron, cinnamon stick, and chopped tomatoes. Tie the cilantro and parsley sprigs in a bunch and add to the pan. Season with 1 1/2 teaspoons salt and freshly ground black pepper to taste. Bring to a gentle boil, cover, and cook over low heat for 25 minutes. Add the carrot to the pan and simmer for an additional 20 minutes. Add the zucchini and peas or fava beans and cook for 15–20 minutes or until the chicken and vegetables are tender.

Meanwhile, to make the spiced couscous, prepare and steam the couscous as directed, either over the stew, over a saucepan of boiling water, or in the microwave oven. Stir the smen or butter through the couscous.

In a saucepan with 1/4 cup water, heat the chickpeas, tossing frequently until the water evaporates. Add to the couscous and stir through.

Pile the couscous on a large, warm platter. Make a well in the center and ladle the chicken and vegetables on top, letting some tumble down the sides. Moisten with some of the broth from the stew. Put about 1 cup of the broth into a bowl and stir in the harissa. Add the harissa-flavored broth to the couscous to keep it moist.

couscous with lamb and seven vegetables .... serves 4–5

THE NUMBER SEVEN IS CONSIDERED AUSPICIOUS IN MOROCCO, HENCE THE SEVEN VEGETABLES IN THIS DISTINCTIVE DISH. THE TURNIPS SHOULD BE YOUNG AND CRISP—DO NOT USE RUTABAGA AS A SUBSTITUTE FOR THE TURNIPS, AS THE FLAVOR IS TOO STRONG.

lamb shoulder	2 lb. 4 oz., boned
olive oil	1/4 cup
onions	2, quartered
garlic	2 cloves, finely chopped
ground turmeric	1/2 teaspoon
paprika	1/2 teaspoon
ground saffron threads	1/4 teaspoon
cilantro	4 sprigs
Italian parsley	4 sprigs
cinnamon stick	1
chopped tomatoes	14-oz. can
freshly ground black pepper	1 1/2 teaspoons
carrots	3, cut into thick sticks
turnips	3 small, peeled and quartered
butternut squash	14 oz.
raisins	1/4 cup
zucchini	4, cut into sticks
chickpeas	15-oz. can, rinsed and drained
couscous	4–5 servings (page 140)
harissa	2–3 teaspoons, to taste

Trim the lamb of excess fat if necessary. Cut the lamb into 3/4-inch cubes. Heat the oil in a large saucepan or the base of a large couscoussier and add the lamb, onion, and garlic. Cook over medium heat, turning the lamb once, just until the lamb loses its red color. Stir in the turmeric, paprika, and saffron and add 3 cups water. Tie the cilantro and parsley in a bunch and add it to the pan, along with the cinnamon stick and tomatoes. Add the pepper and 1 1/2 teaspoons salt to taste. Bring to a gentle boil, cover, and simmer over low heat for 1 hour. Add the carrot and turnip and cook for an additional 20 minutes.

Meanwhile, peel the squash and cut it into 1-inch chunks. Add the squash to the pan, along with the raisins, zucchini, and chickpeas, adding a little water if necessary to almost cover the ingredients. Cook for an additional 20 minutes or until the meat and vegetables are tender.

Prepare and steam the couscous as directed, either over the stew, over a saucepan of boiling water, or in a microwave oven.

Pile the couscous on a deep, heated platter. Make a well in the center. Remove the herbs and cinnamon stick from the stew and ladle the meat and vegetables on top of the couscous, letting some tumble down the sides. Moisten with a little broth from the stew. Pour about 1 cup of the remaining broth into a bowl and stir in the harissa. Add the harissa-flavored broth to the couscous to keep it moist.

dishes from the palace

Moroccan cooking began to take shape in the palaces of the ruling Berber dynasties of the fourteenth century. The lavish court kitchens were the conduit by which new foods and recipes were eventually introduced to household kitchens. Women were always employed as cooks; even today, in the palaces of the reigning monarch and in restaurant kitchens, women still do most of the cooking. Today the Royal Cooking School, set up by King Hussein II in his Rabat Palace complex, still continues the tradition as the training ground for future chefs and household cooks.

Originating in the palaces, the Moroccan *diffa* (banquet) is a showcase of the skills of Moroccan cooks, when the female family members prepare the food. Betrothals, weddings, births, and religious festivals are occasions to celebrate with abundance. Especially lavish *diffas* are given when a Moroccan returns from a pilgrimage to Mecca.

Seated around low, round tables, on divans luxurious with multicolored cushions, guests feast on many little dishes before the *bisteeya* is served in all its glory. This famous squab (or chicken) pie was developed over many years in palace kitchens, and is considered one of the high points of Moroccan cuisine.

Tagines of meat, poultry, and fish follow, including one or more that are sweetened with fruit and honey: chicken, preserved lemon, and olive tagine; chicken with apricots and honey; lamb with eggs and almonds; lamb with dates; beef with apples and raisins; whole fish stuffed with almond-filled dates and finished with an almond crust. Herbs and spice mixes flavor them, orange flower water or rosewater perfume some of them, roasted almonds or sesame seeds are strewn over them. And to follow these, couscous—at least two versions, one sweetened and one containing lamb. Platters of fresh fruit nestled in ice complete the feast, followed by mint tea served with great ceremony.

From palace cooking to the humble Moroccan kitchen—it took a few hundred years, but the road thus traveled has given the cooking of Morocco a formidable reputation.

briouats with goat cheese . . . . makes 24

THESE ARE TRADITIONALLY MADE WITH *WARKHA* PASTRY, FORMED BY DABBING A BALL OF DOUGH ON A HEATED, UPTURNED COPPER PAN UNTIL THE DOUGH BECOMES A FINE, ALMOST TRANSPARENT SHEET. EGG ROLL AND WONTON WRAPPERS CAN BE SUBSTITUTED FOR FRIED PASTRIES AND PHYLLO FOR BAKED PASTRIES.

cheese filling

fresh goat cheese	1 cup
Italian parsley	1/4 cup finely chopped
mint	2 teaspoons finely chopped
paprika	1/2 teaspoon
freshly ground black pepper	1/4 teaspoon
egg	1, lightly beaten
wonton wrappers	24
egg white	1, lightly beaten
oil	for deep-frying

To make the cheese filling, mix the cheese with the parsley, mint, paprika, and black pepper. Taste and add salt if desired. Stir in the beaten egg gradually, adding just enough to retain a fairly stiff mixture—if too loose, the rolls will be difficult to shape.

Put a stack of wonton wrappers in the folds of a dish towel or cover them with plastic wrap to prevent them from drying out. Place a wrapper on the work surface with one corner of the square toward you and brush around the edge with the egg white. Put 2 teaspoons of cheese filling across the corner, just meeting the sides. Roll once, turn each side of the wrapper over the filling, and roll to the end. Place seam side down on a cloth-covered tray. Continue in this manner with the remaining ingredients.

Heat the oil to 350°F or until a cube of bread dropped into the hot oil browns in 15 seconds. Add four *briouats* at a time and fry until golden, turning to brown evenly. Remove with a slotted spoon and drain on paper towels. Serve hot.

Brush around the edge of the wrapper with egg white.

Put 2 teaspoons of the filling on each wrapper and roll up.

mezghaldi of onions
with eggplant .... serves 4

THESE SPICY, CARAMELIZED ONIONS ARE USUALLY SERVED ON THEIR OWN AS AN APPETIZER SALAD, BUT CAN ALSO BE TEAMED WITH CHARBROILED EGGPLANT. USE THEM AS AN ACCOMPANIMENT TO CHARBROILED MEATS OR CHICKEN.

onions	4 medium
olive oil	1/2 cup
ground saffron threads	1/2 teaspoon
ground ginger	1 teaspoon
ground cinnamon	1 teaspoon
ground allspice	1/2 teaspoon
honey	2 tablespoons
long, thin eggplants	9–10

Halve the onions lengthwise and cut them into slender wedges. Put them in a frying pan with a lid, cover with cold water, and bring to a boil. Simmer covered for 5 minutes. Drain the onion in a colander.

Over low heat, add 3 tablespoons of the olive oil to the pan and stir in the saffron, ginger, cinnamon, and allspice. Cook for 1 minute. Increase the heat to medium and return the onion to the pan. Add the honey and 1 1/2 cups water and season with salt and freshly ground black pepper. Stir well, reduce the heat to low, cover, and simmer for 40 minutes. Then uncover and simmer for 10 minutes or until most of the liquid has evaporated.

Wash and dry the eggplants. Leaving the green stalks on, halve them lengthwise and peel off a strip of skin from the underside of each half. Using the remaining oil, brush the eggplant halves on each side. Charbroil or barbecue the eggplants on each side for 3–4 minutes or until they are tender, adjusting the heat so they do not burn.

Arrange the eggplants cut side up on a platter or individual plates and season lightly with salt. Top with the onion and any juices from the pan. Serve hot or warm with crusty bread.

Halve the eggplants lengthwise, leaving the green stalks attached.

Peel a strip of skin from the underside of each eggplant half.

Charbroil or barbecue the eggplant until it is tender.

harira

THIS SOUP IS THE CENTERPIECE OF THE "BREAK FAST" MEAL OF RAMADAN. THE FLAVORFUL LAMB-BASED SOUP IS BOOSTED WITH CHICKPEAS OR LENTILS. IT HAS TO SATISFY HUNGER QUICKLY, SO NOODLES ARE SOMETIMES ADDED, OR IT IS THICKENED WITH YEAST OR FLOUR. VENDORS ALSO SELL IT AS STREET FOOD, LADLED INTO BOWLS.

lamb shoulder steaks	1 lb. 2 oz.
olive oil	3 tablespoons
onions	2 small, chopped
garlic	2 large cloves, crushed
ground cumin	1 1/2 teaspoons
paprika	2 teaspoons
bay leaf	1
tomato paste	3 tablespoons
beef stock	4 cups
chickpeas	2 x 15-oz. cans
chopped tomatoes	1 lb. 12 oz. can
cilantro	1/4 cup finely chopped, plus extra to serve
Italian parsley	1/4 cup finely chopped
flatbread	to serve

Trim the lamb steaks of excess fat and sinew. Cut the lamb into small cubes.

Heat the olive oil in a large heavy-based saucepan or stockpot, add the onion and garlic, and cook over low heat for 5 minutes or until the onion is soft. Add the meat, increase the heat to medium, and stir until the meat changes color.

Add the cumin, paprika, and bay leaf to the pan and cook until fragrant. Add the tomato paste and cook for about 2 minutes, stirring constantly. Add the beef stock to the pan, stir well, and bring to a boil.

Drain and rinse the chickpeas and add to the pan, along with the tomatoes and chopped cilantro and parsley. Stir, then bring to a boil. Reduce the heat and simmer for 2 hours or until the meat is tender. Stir occasionally. Season to taste. Garnish with the extra cilantro and serve with flatbread.

Chickpeas are the most popular legume in Morocco, originating in the Middle East and probably introduced by the Romans. Soaked, unskinned chickpeas are used in soups, while skinned chickpeas are preferred in tagines and stews so that flavors can be absorbed. Soak chickpeas overnight; the next day, lift up handfuls of chickpeas and rub them between your hands to loosen the skins, then skim the skins off as they float. Cover the chickpeas with fresh water and boil for at least an hour, until tender, or add to a stew or soup at the start of cooking. Canned chickpeas may also be used, with skins removed in the same way. If preferred, leave skins on for all recipes.

the spice shop

The Arabs had been involved in the spice trade for centuries before their armies marched forth from Arabia to spread the teachings of Muhammad. When they reached Morocco in the late seventh century, they brought their spices with them and these have been part of the Moroccan kitchen ever since.

In the spice shops of the *souks*, the ground spices—reds, yellows, and all shades of brown—are shaped into smooth mounds in baskets, bins or bowls. Whole spices—buds, bark, quills, nutmegs, cardamom pods and star anise (recently introduced), tears of gum arabic, dried chilies, and fragrant rosebuds—contrast with the elegant piles of the ground spices. The mingling aromas give a promise of what they can do to uplift the forthcoming meal. The eight most important spices for Moroccan cooking are cinnamon, cumin, saffron (sold in small, clear plastic containers to maintain freshness), paprika, turmeric, black pepper, *fefla soudaniya* (similar to cayenne pepper), and ginger. Then there are cloves, allspice, coriander seeds, fenugreek, aniseed, and caraway seeds. As tempting as the aromas might be, Moroccan cooks only purchase spices in small amounts to ensure freshness, taking their purchases home in twisted paper packages to be stored in pottery jars in their kitchens.

Each spice shop has its own *ras el hanout*, which translates as "storekeeper's choice." This mixture may contain as few as ten or as many as twenty-six different ground spices, depending on the whim of the maker. Spices may include pepper, cayenne pepper, lavender,

thyme, rosemary, cumin, ginger, allspice, nutmeg, mace, cardamom, cloves, cinnamon, fenugreek, and grains of paradise, also known as melegueta pepper. Orris root, cubeb pepper, belladonna, rosebuds, hashish, and other ingredients—some not available outside Morocco— might be included, depending of course on the shopkeeper.

For a simplified version of *ras el hanout*, combine ½ teaspoon each of ground cloves and cayenne pepper; 2 teaspoons each of ground allspice, cumin, ginger, turmeric, black pepper, and cardamom; 1 tablespoon each of ground coriander and cinnamon; and 2 freshly grated nutmegs or 1½ tablespoons ground nutmeg in a bowl. Mix thoroughly and place in a clean, dry jar. Seal and store in a cool, dark place and use as directed in recipes. Where the flavor of dried rose petals is required, rosewater has been included in recipes to replace the traditional dried rosebuds used in some *ras el hanout* mixtures.

lamb tagine with dates..serves 6

IN THIS RICH AND LUSCIOUS DISH, THE DRIED DATES ARE PITTED AND USED TO THICKEN THE SAUCE, WHICH CARRIES THEIR FLAVOR THROUGH THE DISH. THE WHOLE DATES USED TO COMPLETE THE DISH ARE LEFT UNPITTED; OTHERWISE THEY CAN DISINTEGRATE.

boneless lamb from shoulder or leg	2 lb. 4 oz.
butter	2 tablespoons, plus 1 tablespoon, extra
onion	1, finely chopped
ground ginger	1 teaspoon
ground cinnamon	1 teaspoon
freshly ground black pepper	1/2 teaspoon
dried dates	1/3 cup, pitted and chopped
ground saffron threads	a pinch
honey	3 tablespoons
lemon juice	3 tablespoons
unpitted fresh or dessert dates	1 cup
preserved lemon	1/2
slivered almonds	1/3 cup

Trim the lamb and cut it into 1-inch cubes. In a large, heavy-based saucepan, melt the butter over low heat, add the onion, and cook gently until softened. Sprinkle in the ground ginger, cinnamon, and black pepper and stir for 1 minute. Increase the heat to high, add the lamb, and stir until the meat changes color. Reduce the heat and add 1 1/2 cups water, the chopped dates, saffron, and 1 teaspoon salt or to taste. Reduce the heat to low, cover, and simmer for 1 1/2 hours, stirring occasionally to prevent the sauce from sticking as the chopped dates cook to a purée.

Stir in the honey and lemon juice and adjust the seasoning. Put the fresh dates on top, cover, and simmer for 10 minutes or until the dates are plump.

Meanwhile, rinse the preserved lemon under cold running water, then remove and discard the pulp. Pat the rind dry with paper towels, and cut into strips. Melt the extra butter in a small frying pan, add the almonds, and brown lightly, stirring often. Tip immediately onto a plate to prevent overbrowning.

Remove the whole dates from the top of the lamb and set them aside with the almonds. Ladle the meat into a serving dish or tagine and sprinkle the dates on top, along with the lemon strips and roasted almonds. Serve hot.

Add the lamb to the onion and spices and cook, stirring.

Put the unpitted dates on top of the lamb mixture.

chicken with preserved
lemon and olives . . . . serves 4

ONE OF THE CLASSIC DISHES OF MOROCCO, CALLED *DJEJ EMSHMEL*, THIS COMBINATION OF SUBTLY SPICED CHICKEN, PRESERVED LEMON, AND OLIVES IS USUALLY SERVED AT BANQUETS. USE UNPITTED GREEN OLIVES; IF THEY ARE BITTER, BLANCH THEM IN BOILING WATER FOR 5 MINUTES BEFORE ADDING TO THE CHICKEN.

preserved lemon	¼
olive oil	¼ cup
chicken	3 lb. 8 oz.
onion	1, chopped
garlic	2 cloves, chopped
chicken stock	2½ cups
ground ginger	½ teaspoon
ground cinnamon	1½ teaspoons
saffron threads	a pinch
unpitted green olives	½ cup
bay leaves	2
chicken livers	2
cilantro	¼ cup chopped

Rinse the preserved lemon under cold running water; remove and discard the pulp. Pat the rind dry with paper towels and cut into strips. Set aside.

Preheat the oven to 350°F. Heat 3 tablespoons of the olive oil in a large frying pan, add the chicken, and brown on all sides. Place in a deep baking dish.

Heat the remaining oil, add the onion and garlic, and cook over medium heat for 3–4 minutes or until the onion is softened. Add the chicken stock, ginger, cinnamon, saffron, olives, bay leaves, and preserved lemon strips, then pour the sauce around the chicken in the dish. Bake for 1½ hours or until cooked through, adding a little more water or stock if the sauce gets too dry. Baste the chicken during cooking.

Remove the chicken from the dish, cover with foil, and set aside. Pour the contents of the baking dish into a frying pan, add the chicken livers, and mash them into the sauce as they cook. Cook for 5–6 minutes or until the sauce has reduced and thickened. Add the chopped cilantro. Cut the chicken into pieces and serve with the sauce.

Remove the bitter pulp from the preserved lemon.

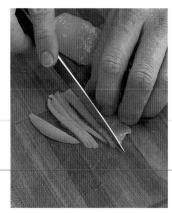

Cut the preserved lemon rind into thin strips.

chicken with
apricots and honey . . . . serves 4

WHOLE CHICKENS AND CHICKENS CUT INTO PORTIONS ARE COMMON IN MOROCCO. HOWEVER, BONELESS, SKINLESS CHICKEN BREASTS ARE USED IN THIS DISH TO DECREASE THE COOKING TIME. WHEN FRESH APRICOTS ARE NOT IN SEASON, CANNED APRICOTS ARE A GOOD ALTERNATIVE.

chicken breasts	4 x 6 oz.
butter	3 tablespoons
ground cinnamon	1 teaspoon
ground ginger	1 teaspoon
freshly ground black pepper	1/4 teaspoon
cayenne pepper	1/8 teaspoon
onion	1, sliced
chicken stock	1 cup
cilantro	6 sprigs tied in a bunch
apricots	8 medium (or 15-oz. can apricot halves in natural juice)
honey	3 tablespoons
couscous	4–5 servings (page 140)
slivered almonds	3 tablespoons, roasted

Trim the chicken breasts of any fat or gristle. Melt the butter in a large covered frying pan. Add the spices and stir over low heat for about 1 minute. Increase the heat to medium and add the chicken breasts. Turn them in the spiced butter and cook on each side for 1 minute without allowing the spices to burn.

Add the onion to the pan around the chicken and cook for 5 minutes, stirring the onion and turning the chicken occasionally. Add the stock and cilantro sprigs and season if desired. Reduce the heat to low, cover, and simmer for 5 minutes, turning the chicken once.

Wash and halve the apricots and remove the pits. Place them, cut side down, around the chicken and drizzle with the honey. Cover and simmer for 7–8 minutes, turning the apricots after 5 minutes. Remove the chicken to a plate, cover, and allow to sit for 2–3 minutes. Slice each breast diagonally.

Prepare and steam the couscous as directed, either over a saucepan of boiling water or in the microwave. Put the hot couscous on serving plates and top with the sliced chicken. Remove the cilantro sprigs from the sauce and spoon the sauce and apricots over the chicken. Sprinkle with the almonds and serve hot.

Turn the chicken breasts in the spiced butter.

Drizzle the honey over the apricot halves in the pan.

Turn the apricot halves once during cooking.

Allow the chicken breasts to sit, then slice them diagonally.

three ways with citrus

MOROCCO'S CLIMATE IS IDEAL FOR CITRUS FRUITS, ESPECIALLY ORANGES AND LEMONS—BOTH ARE REVERED AND RELISHED. ORANGES ARE COMBINED WITH INGREDIENTS SUCH AS DATES, RADISHES, OLIVES, OR CARROTS TO CREATE COOLING SALADS, OR ARE SIMPLY SLICED AND SPRINKLED WITH ORANGE FLOWER WATER, SUGAR, AND CINNAMON. FRESH LEMONS MAKE A TART BUT APPETITE-STIMULATING SALAD THAT COMPLEMENTS SWEET SALADS AND TAGINES.

lemon, parsley, and onion salad

Peel 6 lemons with a sharp knife, making sure that all the pith and fine membranes are removed. Cut the lemons into ½-inch-thick slices and remove the seeds. Dice the lemon slices and put them in a bowl. Halve 1 small red onion, then slice it thinly. Chop 2 large handfuls of Italian parsley. Add the onion and parsley to the lemons, along with 1 teaspoon salt and 1 teaspoon superfine sugar. Toss and set aside for 10 minutes. Just before serving, add a light sprinkling of freshly ground black pepper. Serve this salad with fish or as a refreshing, tart contrast to tagines that contain fruit. Serves 6–8.

orange and radish salad

Wash and dry 3 sweet oranges, then cut off the tops and bases. Cut the peel off using a sharp knife, removing all traces of pith and cutting through the outer membranes to expose the flesh. Holding the oranges over a small bowl to catch the juice, segment them by cutting between the membranes. Remove the seeds from the orange segments, then put the segments in the bowl. Squeeze the remains of the oranges into the bowl. Drain the orange segments, reserving the orange juice, and return the segments to the bowl. Set the juice aside. Wash 12 red radishes and trim the roots. Slice thinly using a mandolin or vegetable slicer. Add to the orange segments. Put 3 tablespoons of the reserved orange juice in a small bowl, add 4 teaspoons lemon juice, 2 teaspoons superfine sugar, 3 tablespoons olive oil, and a pinch of salt. Beat well and pour over the salad. Sprinkle with 4 teaspoons orange flower water, toss lightly, and then cover and chill for 15 minutes. Transfer to a serving bowl, sprinkle the top lightly with ground cinnamon, and sprinkle with small mint leaves. Serves 4.

orange and date salad

Wash and dry 6 sweet oranges, then cut off the tops and bases. Cut the peel off with a sharp knife, removing all traces of pith and cutting through the outer membranes to expose the flesh. Holding the oranges over a bowl to catch the juice, segment them by cutting between the membranes. Remove the seeds and put the segments in the bowl. Squeeze the remains of the oranges over the bowl to extract all the juice. Add 2 teaspoons orange flower water and stir gently to combine. Cover with plastic wrap and refrigerate until chilled. Thinly slice 8 pitted dates lengthwise. Lightly roast ¾ cup slivered almonds. Place the orange segments and juice on a large, flat dish and sprinkle the dates and slivered almonds on the top. Sprinkle small mint leaves over the orange segments. Serve chilled. Serves 4–6.

tagine of beef
with apples and raisins . . . . serves 6

THIS IS A ROBUST BEEF TAGINE THAT IS SERVED WHEN APPLES ARE IN SEASON. ADDING RAISINS, SPICES, AND HONEY MELLOWS THE TARTNESS OF THE FRUIT. FOR A REALLY AUTHENTIC FLAVOR, CHOOSE A THICK, THYME-FLAVORED HONEY IF POSSIBLE.

chuck or blade steak	2 lb. 4 oz.
oil	3 tablespoons
butter	3 tablespoons
onion	1 medium, sliced
ground saffron threads	1/4 teaspoon
ground ginger	1/2 teaspoon
ground cinnamon	1 teaspoon, plus 1/2 teaspoon extra
cilantro	4 sprigs tied in a bunch
raisins	1 cup
honey	1/4 cup
tart apples, such as Granny Smith	3, halved, cored, and cut into thick wedges
sesame seeds	4 teaspoons, roasted

Trim the beef and cut it into 1-inch cubes. Heat half the oil and half the butter in a heavy-based saucepan over high heat and brown the beef in batches. Remove to a dish when cooked. Add the remaining oil as needed.

Reduce the heat to medium, add the onion, and cook for 5 minutes to soften. Add the saffron, ginger, and cinnamon and cook for 1 minute. Stir in 1 1/2 cups water, 1 1/2 teaspoons salt, and a generous grinding of black pepper. Return the beef to the pan, along with the cilantro. Cover and simmer over low heat for 1 1/2 hours. Add the raisins and 4 teaspoons of honey. Cover and simmer for an additional 30 minutes or until the meat is tender.

Heat the remaining butter in a frying pan and cook the apples for 10 minutes, turning often. Drizzle with the remaining honey, dust with the extra cinnamon, and cook for 5 minutes or until glazed and softened. Transfer the meat and sauce to a serving dish, arrange the apple on top, and sprinkle with the sesame seeds.

Hillsides covered with wild thyme and blossoming fruit trees—especially citrus—lure bees to perform their intricate work, often capturing the essence of the blossom in the honey produced. Thyme-flavored honey is thick with a distinctive flavor just right for adding to tagines; orange blossom honey adds its delicate flavor and aroma to sweet pastries. Light, crumpetlike semolina pancakes, spread with butter while hot and drizzled with ambrosial honey, are a favorite breakfast treat. Be careful when heating honey in which to dip sweet pastries, as the honey can scorch easily. Adding a little water can help avoid this.

bisteeya .... serves 6–8

THIS CLASSIC SQUAB (OR CHICKEN) PIE IS TRADITIONALLY ENCLOSED IN MOROCCAN *WARKHA* PASTRY, THEN FRIED, DUSTED WITH POWDERED SUGAR, AND DECORATED WITH LINES OF CINNAMON IN A DIAMOND PATTERN. HOWEVER, PHYLLO PASTRY CAN BE USED INSTEAD.

smen or butter	1 cup
chicken	3 lb. 5 oz., quartered
	(or 3 x 1 lb. 2 oz. squab, halved)
red onions	2 large, finely chopped
garlic	3 cloves, crushed
cinnamon stick	1
ground ginger	1 teaspoon
ground cumin	1 1/2 teaspoons
cayenne pepper	1/4 teaspoon
ground turmeric	1/2 teaspoon
chicken stock	2 cups
saffron threads	a large pinch, soaked in
	3 tablespoons warm water
lemon juice	4 teaspoons
Italian parsley	2 large handfuls, chopped
cilantro	2 large handfuls, chopped leaves
eggs	5, lightly beaten
almonds	2/3 cup, roasted, finely chopped
confectioners' sugar	1/4 cup, plus extra to serve
ground cinnamon	1 teaspoon, plus extra to serve
phyllo pastry	12 sheets

Preheat the oven to 315°F. Melt 10 tablespoons of the smen or butter in a large flameproof casserole dish over medium heat and brown the chicken well. Set aside. Add the onion and cook until golden. Stir in the garlic and spices, then stir in the stock and saffron water. Add the chicken and turn to coat. Cover and bake, turning occasionally, for 1 hour or until cooked. Add a little extra water if needed. Discard the cinnamon stick. Drain the chicken, remove the meat from the bones, and cut it into small pieces. Increase the oven temperature to 350°F.

Add the lemon juice and herbs to the sauce. Cook over high heat for 10 minutes or until thick. With the heat on very low, gradually stir in the beaten egg. Continue stirring until scrambled. Remove from the heat. Add the chicken and season to taste.

Mix the almonds with the sugar and cinnamon. Melt the remaining smen. Brush a 6-cup deep pie or baking dish with the smen. Put a phyllo sheet over the dish so the edges overhang; brush with smen. Repeat with seven more sheets, brushing with smen, slightly overlapping the sheets to give a pinwheel effect. Fill with the chicken mixture. Fold four of the phyllo flaps back over, brush with smen, and sprinkle with the almond mixture. Fold the remaining flaps over and tuck the edges into the dish. Brush four phyllo sheets with smen, cut into 6-inch squares, and scrunch into "flowers" to cover the pie. Bake for 1 hour or until golden. Serve sprinkled with the combined extra sugar and cinnamon.

Overlap the phyllo in the pie dish, brushing with the smen.

Sprinkle the almond mixture over the phyllo.

Scrunch the phyllo sheets into "flowers" to cover the pie.

mechoui . . . . serves 6

THIS HOME-COOKED VERSION OF *MECHOUI* IS A GOOD INDICATION OF THE SUCCULENCE OF SLOW-COOKED LAMB. THE BASTING IS IMPORTANT TO KEEP THE MEAT MOIST AND TO COOK IT TO MELT-IN-THE-MOUTH TENDERNESS. IF THE LAMB BROWNS TOO QUICKLY, MOVE IT TO THE CENTER OF THE OVEN AND TURN IT OCCASIONALLY.

leg of lamb	5 lb.
butter	5 tablespoons, softened at room temperature
garlic	3 cloves, crushed
ground coriander	1 tablespoon
paprika	1 teaspoon
ground cumin	2 tablespoons
coarse salt	2 teaspoons

Preheat the oven to 425°F. With a small, sharp knife, cut small, deep slits in the top and sides of the lamb.

Mix the butter, garlic, coriander, paprika, 2 teaspoons of the cumin, and ¼ teaspoon salt in a bowl to form a smooth paste. With the back of a spoon, rub the paste all over the lamb, then use your fingers to spread the paste evenly, making sure all the lamb is covered.

Put the lamb bone-side down in a deep baking dish and place on the top rack of the oven. Bake for 10 minutes, then baste the lamb and return it to the oven. Reduce the oven temperature to 315°F. Bake for 3¼ hours, basting every 20–30 minutes to ensure the lamb stays tender and flavorful.

Carve the lamb into chunky pieces. Mix the remaining cumin with the coarse salt and serve on the side for dipping.

Berber in origin, *mechoui* is spit-roasted lamb at its best. When Berbers have their *moussems* (festivals), the roasting of the lamb is the highlight of their celebrations. A mixture of spices (cumin, coriander, and paprika), crushed garlic, and salt is rubbed over the lamb and pushed into incisions, then the whole lamb is rubbed generously with herbed smen. Spit-roasted over a glowing charcoal fire, the lamb is frequently basted with the smen to keep it moist and succulent. The lamb is cooked until it is butter-soft so that morsels can be pulled off with the fingers. Cumin mixed with salt is the traditional accompaniment.

three ways with quince

QUINCE IS TEAMED WITH LAMB AND POULTRY FOR SWEET AND SOUR DISHES OF PERSIAN ORIGIN; THE MOROCCAN VERSIONS ARE MORE HIGHLY SPICED. WHILE MOROCCANS DO NOT MAKE QUINCE PASTE, IT IS USED IN ONE OF THE RECIPES BELOW FOR THE FLAVOR OF QUINCE OUT OF SEASON. POACHING QUINCE WITH THE SKIN AND CORE INTACT GIVES A ROSY HUE TO THE FRUIT, SOMETHING THAT IS OTHERWISE DIFFICULT TO ACHIEVE UNLESS THE QUINCE IS SLOWLY COOKED FOR 2 HOURS OR MORE, BY WHICH TIME IT IS OVERCOOKED.

lamb tagine with quince

Cut 3 lb. 5 oz. lamb shoulder into 1¼-inch pieces. Put the lamb in a heavy-based, flameproof casserole dish. Roughly chop 2 large handfuls of cilantro leaves and add to the dish, along with 1 large diced onion, ½ teaspoon ground ginger, ½ teaspoon cayenne pepper, ¼ teaspoon ground saffron threads, 1 teaspoon ground coriander, 1 cinnamon stick, and some salt and freshly ground black pepper. Cover with cold water and bring to a boil over medium heat. Lower the heat and simmer, partly covered, for 1½ hours or until the lamb is tender. While the lamb is cooking, peel, core, and quarter 2 medium quinces. Melt 3 tablespoons butter in a heavy-based frying pan over medium heat and cook the quinces and 1 large diced onion for 15 minutes or until lightly golden. When the lamb has been cooking for 1 hour, add the quince mixture, ½ cup dried apricots, and 4 teaspoons superfine sugar. Taste the sauce and adjust the seasoning if necessary. Transfer to a warm serving dish and sprinkle with cilantro leaves. Serve with couscous or rice. Serves 4–6.

chicken and quince tagine

You will need a 3 lb. 5 oz. chicken that has been cut into quarters. Cut diagonal slashes in the fleshy parts of the chicken pieces such as the breasts, legs, and thighs. Rub 2 teaspoons *ras el hanout* into the chicken, cover, and leave to marinate for 20 minutes. Heat 3 tablespoons oil in a large covered frying pan over medium heat. Add the chicken pieces in batches, skin side down, and brown lightly for 2 minutes, then turn them over and cook for an additional 2 minutes. Remove to a plate. Add 1 sliced onion to the pan and cook for 5 minutes or until soft. Add 1 cup chicken stock, stir well to lift the browned juices off the base of the pan, then return the chicken to the pan. Season lightly with salt if necessary. Reduce the heat to low, then cover and simmer for 45 minutes, turning the chicken occasionally. When the chicken is tender, cut ⅓ cup quince paste into thin slices, and then add it to the pan juices, mashing it with a fork until it melts into the liquid. Stir in 4 teaspoons lemon juice and 2 teaspoons rosewater and simmer for 1 minute. Serve the chicken with the quince sauce and spiced carrots (page 30). Serves 4.

poached quinces with rosewater

Wash 2 medium quinces well and cut into quarters. Place in a saucepan and cover with water. Bring to a boil, then cover and simmer over low heat for 40 minutes or until almost tender and beginning to color. Drain in a fine sieve over a bowl and return the liquid to the pan. Add ¾ cup sugar and the thinly peeled zest of ½ lemon to the pan. Stir until the sugar has dissolved, then leave to simmer gently. Meanwhile, pull the skin from the quince quarters, remove the cores, and halve each quarter. Place the quince slices in the syrup with 4 teaspoons rosewater. Simmer uncovered for an additional 30 minutes or until the quinces are tender and have a rosy hue. Remove the lemon zest and serve warm or chilled. Serves 4.

lamb with
eggs and almonds...... serves 6

CALLED *TAFAYA*, THIS TAGINE IS SERVED AT CELEBRATIONS THROUGHOUT MOROCCO. TO GIVE THE DISH A FESTIVE TOUCH, SOME COOKS DIP THE SHELLED, BOILED EGGS IN SAFFRON-INFUSED HOT WATER, WHICH COLORS THEM AND GIVES THEM EXTRA FLAVOR.

lamb shoulder chops	2 lb. 12 oz.
olive oil	1/4 cup
onions	2, coarsely grated
garlic	3 cloves, finely chopped
ground ginger	2 teaspoons
ground saffron threads	1/4 teaspoon
cilantro	1/4 cup chopped plus extra to serve
butter	3 tablespoons
blanched almonds	1 cup
eggs	6, hard-boiled and halved

Trim the excess fat from the chops. Heat half the oil in a large saucepan over high heat and brown the lamb in batches, removing to a dish when cooked. Add a little more oil as needed.

Reduce the heat to low, add the remaining oil and the onions, and cook for 5 minutes or until the onions have softened. Add the garlic and ginger and cook for a few seconds. Pour in 1 1/2 cups water and stir to lift the browned juices off the base of the pan. Return the lamb to the pan, along with the saffron, 1 teaspoon salt, and a good grinding of black pepper. Cover and simmer over low heat for 1 1/4 hours, then stir in the cilantro and cook for an additional 15 minutes or until the lamb is tender.

Meanwhile, melt the butter in a frying pan over medium heat and fry the almonds until golden, tossing frequently. Remove immediately.

Arrange the lamb in a serving dish, spoon the sauce over, and arrange the eggs on top. Sprinkle with the roasted almonds and extra cilantro.

It takes the stigmas of two thousand blooms of the *Crocus sativus* to produce 2 tablespoons of dried saffron threads, making it the world's most expensive spice. Introduced by the Arabs via Moorish Spain, it is now grown, harvested, and processed in Morocco. Threads and ground saffron are used for flavor and color. The threads should be steeped in liquid before use or added dry to tagines and soups during cooking. To make your own ground saffron, lightly roast the threads in a dry, heated frying pan and pound in a mortar with a pestle. Where a recipe calls for a pinch, use as much as sits on the very tip of a knife, as fingertips would take more than needed.

almond-crusted fish with prunes............................serves 4

THIS FRIED FISH STAYS MOIST AND SUCCULENT IN ITS DELICATELY FLAVORED ALMOND CRUST. FISH BAKED WITH AN ALMOND CRUST IS A SPECIALTY OF THE COASTAL CITY OF SAFI. PRUNES ARE ALSO USED WITH FISH, AS A STUFFING, OR IN A DELICIOUS SPICY SAUCE.

white fish fillets, such as blue eye cod, snapper, hake, or sea bass	4 x 7 oz.
pitted prunes	24
blanched almonds	24, lightly roasted
butter	2 tablespoons
onions	2 medium, sliced
ground ginger	3/4 teaspoon
ground cinnamon	3/4 teaspoon
freshly ground black pepper	1/8 teaspoon
ground saffron threads	1/8 teaspoon
sugar	1 1/2 teaspoons
lemon juice	1 tablespoon
orange flower water	1 tablespoon
egg	1
ground almonds	1 cup
smen or ghee	1/4–1/3 cup
lemon wedges	to serve

Choose center-cut fish fillets no more than 1 1/4 inches thick at the thickest part. Remove the skin (if present) and season lightly with salt. Set aside. Stuff each prune with a whole roasted almond and set aside.

Melt the butter in a covered frying pan and add the onions. Cook for about 10 minutes over low heat, stirring often until the onion is soft and golden. Add 1/2 teaspoon each of the ground ginger and cinnamon, a pinch of salt, and the black pepper. Stir and cook for a few seconds. Pour in 1 cup water and stir in the saffron. Cover and simmer gently for 5 minutes, then add the stuffed prunes, sugar, lemon juice, and orange flower water and stir gently. Cover and simmer for 15 minutes or until the prunes are plump.

Meanwhile, beat the egg in a shallow dish with the remaining ground ginger, ground cinnamon, and 1/4 teaspoon salt. Spread the ground almonds in a flat dish. Dip the fish into the beaten egg, drain briefly, and coat on all sides with the ground almonds. Place on a tray lined with waxed paper.

In a large nonstick frying pan over medium to high heat, melt the smen or ghee (the depth of the smen should be about 1/4 inch). Add the coated fish, reduce the heat to medium, and cook for 2 minutes. Then turn and cook for an additional 2 minutes or until golden and just cooked through. Do not allow the almond coating to burn. If you have to remove the fish before it is cooked through, place it on top of the onion and prune mixture, cover, and simmer gently for 2–3 minutes, taking care that the coating does not become too moist on top. Serve the fish immediately with lemon wedges, and the onion and prune sauce poured on top.

Press a roasted almond into each of the prunes.

Dip the fish in the egg, then coat it with the ground almonds.

three ways with rice

RICE IS NOT WIDELY USED IN MAINSTREAM MOROCCAN COOKING APART FROM RICE PUDDING (PAGE 188) AND ITS VARIATIONS—SUCH AS USING THE THICK PUDDING AS A FILLING FOR FRIED *BRIOUATS* (SWEET PASTRIES SERVED AS A "BREAK FAST" FOOD DURING RAMADAN). HOWEVER, IN TETUÁN, ONCE THE CAPITAL OF SPANISH MOROCCO, RICE IS FEATURED MORE FREQUENTLY. MOROCCANS USUALLY STEAM THE RICE IN THE SAME WAY AS COUSCOUS, ONLY COVERED—A VERY LENGTHY PROCESS.

saffron rice

Wash 2½ cups long-grain rice in a sieve until the water runs clear, then drain well. Bring 3½ cups water to a boil and add ½ teaspoon crushed saffron threads. Allow to infuse for 20 minutes. Heat 3 tablespoons olive oil in a heavy-based saucepan and add the rice, stirring well so that all the rice is coated evenly in the oil. Add the saffron water and ¼ teaspoon salt and stir well. Bring to a boil and boil for 1 minute. Cover with a tight-fitting lid, then reduce the heat to as low as possible and cook for 10–12 minutes or until all the water has been absorbed. Steam tunnels will form holes on the surface. Turn off the heat, then leave the pan covered for at least 10 minutes. Add 1½ tablespoons butter, fluff lightly with a fork, and serve. Serves 6.

rice stuffing for chicken

Cook 1 chopped onion in 3 tablespoons olive oil in a saucepan over medium heat until soft, about 5 minutes. Add ½ cup short-grain rice and cook, stirring occasionally until the rice is opaque. Add 2 peeled, chopped tomatoes, 3 tablespoons chopped Italian parsley, 2 teaspoons chopped mint, ½ teaspoon paprika, a pinch each of cayenne pepper and sugar, and 1½ cups chicken stock. Stir well and bring to a boil. Cover and simmer over low heat for 12 minutes or until the rice is almost cooked and the liquid has been absorbed. When cool, use to stuff two chickens for roasting, packing the stuffing loosely. If only one chicken is cooked, stir a little more water into the remaining stuffing in the saucepan, cook over low heat until tender, and serve with the chicken. Makes enough stuffing for 2 chickens.

Swiss chard with rice

Trim the ends of 8 Swiss chard stalks. Wash well and cut the stalks from the leaves. Slice the stalks thickly and roughly shred the leaves. Heat ⅓ cup olive oil in a large saucepan and add 1 chopped onion. Cook over low heat for 5 minutes or until soft. Stir in the Swiss chard stalks and 1 teaspoon paprika and cook for 5 more minutes. Add the Swiss chard leaves, 3 tablespoons each of chopped cilantro and Italian parsley, ½ cup short-grain rice, and ½ cup water. Increase the heat and stir until the Swiss chard begins to wilt. Reduce the heat to low, add 2 tablespoons lemon juice, and stir well. Cover and simmer for 25 minutes or until the rice is tender, stirring occasionally. Season to taste and serve hot as a vegetable accompaniment. Serves 4.

saffron rice

trout stuffed with dates . . . . serves 4

THE MARRIAGE OF DATES WITH FISH IS A TIME-HONORED PRACTICE IN MOROCCO. TRADITIONALLY THE STUFFED FISH WOULD BE COOKED IN A TAGINE, BUT WITH DOMESTIC OVENS NOW MORE WIDELY AVAILABLE, IT IS OFTEN OVEN-BAKED. THE FOIL WRAPPING KEEPS THE FISH MOIST.

trout	4 medium
dates	3/4 cup, chopped
rice	1/4 cup cooked
onion	1, finely chopped
cilantro	1/3 cup chopped
ground ginger	1/4 teaspoon
ground cinnamon	1/4 teaspoon, plus extra to serve
blanched almonds	1/3 cup roughly chopped
butter	3 tablespoons, softened

Preheat the oven to 350°F. Rinse the trout under cold running water and pat them dry with paper towels. Season lightly with salt and freshly ground black pepper.

Combine the dates, cooked rice, half the onion, the cilantro, ginger, cinnamon, almonds, and half the butter in a bowl. Season well with salt and freshly ground black pepper.

Spoon the stuffing into the fish cavities and place each fish on a well-greased double sheet of foil. Brush the fish with the remaining butter, season with salt and freshly ground black pepper, and divide the remaining onion among the four packages. Wrap the fish neatly and seal the edges of the foil. Place the packages on a large baking sheet and bake for 15–20 minutes or until cooked to your liking. Serve dusted with ground cinnamon.

While the coastal regions of Morocco benefit from a plentiful supply of seafood, inland dwellers depend on freshwater fish, as the freshness of ingredients is of paramount importance to cooks. Salmon (sea) trout and shad (*alose*) are two fish that enter the rivers from the Atlantic to spawn, with the shad regarded as better for eating at this stage. In Fez, fish such as shad caught in the Sebou River feature on banquet menus, baked with dates stuffed with a ground almond paste. Both shad and salmon trout have small bones, especially the shad, and care should be taken when eating; this is where eating with the hand is such an advantage, as it is easier to feel the bones.

fish with harissa and olives

THE SPICY TOMATO SAUCE TAKES ON QUITE A BITE WITH THE ADDITION OF HARISSA—ADD IT WITH CAUTION IF YOU HAVE NOT USED IT BEFORE. IF YOU DO NOT HAVE HARISSA, ADD 1 TEASPOON OF FINELY CHOPPED RED CHILI OR A PINCH OF CAYENNE PEPPER. IF THE SUGGESTED FISH TYPES ARE UNAVAILABLE, OTHER SUITABLE FISH ARE HAKE AND SEA BASS.

all-purpose flour	for dusting
olive oil	1/3 cup
white fish fillets, such as blue-eye cod, snapper, or perch	4
onion	1, chopped
garlic	2 cloves, crushed
chopped tomatoes	14-oz. can
harissa	2 teaspoons or to taste
bay leaves	2
cinnamon stick	1
black olives	1 cup
lemon juice	4 teaspoons
Italian parsley	3 tablespoons chopped

Season the flour with salt and freshly ground black pepper. Heat half the olive oil in a heavy-based frying pan. Dust the fish fillets with the seasoned flour and add to the pan. Cook the fish over medium heat for 2 minutes on each side or until golden. Transfer to a plate.

Add the remaining olive oil to the pan and cook the onion and garlic for 3–4 minutes or until softened. Add the tomatoes, harissa, bay leaves, and cinnamon stick. Cook for 10 minutes or until the sauce has thickened. Season to taste with salt and freshly ground black pepper.

Return the fish to the pan, add the olives, and cover the fish with the sauce. Remove the bay leaves and cinnamon stick and cook for 2 minutes or until the fish is tender. Add the lemon juice and parsley and serve.

Dust the fish fillets with the seasoned flour before cooking.

Cook the fish fillets over medium heat until golden.

couscous

Couscous and instant couscous both require steaming for best results. For 4–5 servings, put 1³/₄ cups couscous in a large, shallow bowl and cover with water. Stir and pour the water off immediately through a strainer, returning the grains to the bowl. Leave for 15 minutes to swell, then rake with your fingers to separate the grains.

Line a steamer or couscoussier with two layers of cheesecloth, add the couscous, and put the steamer over boiling stew or water, making sure the steamer does not touch the liquid. If it does not fit snugly, put a folded strip of foil between the steamer and the pan. Steam uncovered for 20 minutes, forking through the couscous occasionally. Turn into the bowl. Stir ¹/₂ teaspoon salt into ¹/₃ cup cold water. Add 2 tablespoons chopped butter to the couscous and sprinkle with the salted water. Toss through the couscous, and when cool enough, lightly rub handfuls of couscous to break up lumps. Cover and set aside. Twenty minutes before the stew is cooked, return the couscous to the lined steamer and replace over the boiling stew. Fluff up occasionally with a fork.

To cook in the microwave, put the swollen couscous in a 12-cup ceramic dish. Stir ¹/₂ teaspoon salt into 1 cup water. Sprinkle a third of the water over the couscous, cover, and microwave on full power for 3 minutes. Add 2 tablespoons chopped butter and fluff up with a fork. Repeat twice more with the remaining water and fluff with the fork each time. Uncover and fluff up again before serving.

couscous with lamb and raisins

THIS IS ONE OF THE SWEET COUSCOUS DISHES SERVED AT *DIFFAS* (BANQUETS), THE SWEETNESS COMING FROM THE ADDITION OF RICH-TASTING RAISINS. THE LAMB SHANK MEAT COOKS TO MELTING TENDERNESS, BUT OTHER LAMB CUTS CAN BE USED, SUCH AS THICKLY CUT SHOULDER CHOPS.

onions	3
butter	4 tablespoons
lamb shanks	3
ground turmeric	1/2 teaspoon
ground ginger	1 1/2 teaspoons
freshly ground black pepper	1 teaspoon
ground saffron threads	1/4 teaspoon
cayenne pepper	a pinch
cilantro	3 sprigs
Italian parsley	3 sprigs
chickpeas	15-oz. can
raisins	3/4 cup
couscous	4–5 servings (page 140)

Quarter 2 of the onions. Halve and slice the remaining onion and set aside. Heat the butter in a large saucepan or the base of a large couscoussier. Add the lamb shanks, onion quarters, turmeric, ginger, black pepper, saffron, and cayenne pepper. Stir over low heat for 1 minute. Add 2 cups water. Tie the cilantro and parsley sprigs in a bunch and add to the pan with 1 teaspoon salt. Bring to a gentle boil, then cover and simmer over low heat for 1 3/4–2 hours or until the lamb is very tender.

Meanwhile, drain the chickpeas and put them in a large bowl with cold water to cover. Lift up handfuls of chickpeas and rub them between your hands to loosen the skins. Run more water into the bowl, stir well, and let the skins float to the top, then skim them off. Repeat until all the skins have been removed. Drain the chickpeas and set aside.

When the lamb is cooked, lift the shanks from the broth and strip off the meat. Discard the bones and cut the meat into pieces. Return the meat to the pan, along with the chickpeas, reserved onion, and the raisins. Cover and cook for 20 minutes, adding a little more water to the pan if necessary.

Prepare and steam the couscous as directed, either over the stew or a saucepan of boiling water, or in a microwave.

Pile the couscous on a large, warm platter and make a well in the center. Remove and discard the cilantro and parsley sprigs, then ladle the lamb mixture into the hollow. Moisten with some of the broth and put the remaining broth in a bowl, which can be added as needed.

Rub the chickpeas between your hands to loosen the skins.

Strip the tender meat off the lamb shanks.

roast chicken with
couscous stuffing . . . . serves 4–6

MOROCCAN COOKS USUALLY STEAM STUFFED CHICKEN OR COOK IT WHOLE IN A TAGINE. TO BROWN IT, THEY REMOVE IT FROM ITS SAUCE IF NECESSARY, AND FRY IT ON ALL SIDES IN A FRYING PAN. THE FOLLOWING RECIPE IS FOR OVEN-ROASTED CHICKEN.

chicken	3 lb. 8 oz.
paprika	2 teaspoons
butter	2 tablespoons, softened
chicken stock	1 cup

stuffing

couscous	3/4 cup
raisins	1/3 cup
butter	2 tablespoons, diced
honey	4 teaspoons
ground cinnamon	1/2 teaspoon
blanched almonds	1/4 cup, lightly roasted

Preheat the oven to 350°F. Rinse the cavity of the chicken and dry with paper towels. Season the chicken on the outside and sprinkle with the paprika. Rub it into the skin.

To make the stuffing, put the couscous in a glass or ceramic covered casserole dish and mix in the raisins, butter, honey, and cinnamon. Pour in 1/2 cup boiling water, stir well, and set aside until the water has been absorbed. Fluff up the grains with a fork to break up the lumps. Cover and microwave on high for 2 1/2 minutes. Fluff up again with the fork, add the almonds, and toss through. Alternatively, follow the directions on the packet to prepare the couscous, adding the extra ingredients.

Spoon half the stuffing into the cavity of the chicken, packing it in loosely. Tie the legs together and tuck the wing tips under.

Spread a little of the softened butter in the base of a baking dish. Put the chicken in the dish breast side up, spread with the remaining butter, and pour the stock into the dish. Roast for 1 1/2–1 3/4 hours, basting often with the liquid in the baking dish. Remove to a platter and set aside in a warm place for 15 minutes before carving. The pan juices may be strained over the chicken. Reheat the remaining couscous stuffing and serve with the chicken, along with orange and date salad (page 120) or orange and carrot salad (page 30).

Pack the stuffing into the chicken and tie the legs together.

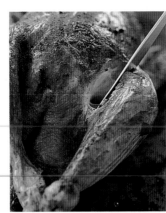

Roast the chicken until tender, basting with the cooking juices.

sweet couscous

SWEET COUSCOUS IS OFTEN SERVED AS THE FINAL SAVORY DISH OF A BANQUET. AS IT IS A POPULAR DISH AT PALACE BANQUETS, THE MORE EXPENSIVE NUTS—PISTACHIOS AND PINE NUTS—ARE OFTEN USED, ALONG WITH THE TRADITIONAL ALMONDS AND WALNUTS.

pistachio nuts, pine nuts and blanched almonds	1/2 cup, combined
dried apricots	1/4 cup
couscous	1 1/3 cups
superfine sugar	1/4 cup, plus 3 tablespoons extra
unsalted butter	6 tablespoons, softened
ground cinnamon	1/2 teaspoon
milk	1 1/2 cups, hot

Preheat the oven to 315°F. Spread the nuts on a cookie sheet and bake for about 5 minutes or until lightly golden. Allow to cool, then coarsely chop and place in a bowl. Julienne the apricots. Add to the bowl with the nuts and toss to combine.

Put the couscous and sugar in a large bowl and cover with 1 cup boiling water. Stir well, then add the butter and a pinch of salt. Stir until the butter melts. Cover with a dish towel and set aside for 10 minutes. (Alternatively, prepare and steam or microwave the couscous as described on page 140.) Fluff the grains with a fork, then toss with half the fruit and nut mixture.

To serve, pile the warm couscous in the center of a platter. Arrange the remaining nut mixture around the edge. Combine the extra sugar and the cinnamon in a small bowl and serve separately for sprinkling. Pass around the hot milk in a pitcher for guests to help themselves.

While there are other members of the family Pistacia, *Pistacia vera*, native to Western Asia, is the species that produces the pistachio nut. The Romans introduced the pistachio tree to North Africa, but it has yet to rival the almond in popularity in Morocco. The fruit of the tree resembles green olives, with a reddish blush when ripe. When the outer covering is removed, the beige, smooth-shelled nut is already partly opened, exposing the kernel (termed *khandan*, or "smiling," in Iran—the most prolific producer of pistachios). The pistachio nut itself has the advantage of being green, or green-tinged, adding color as well as its delicate flavor to dessert dishes and pastries.

sweets, pastries,
and drinks

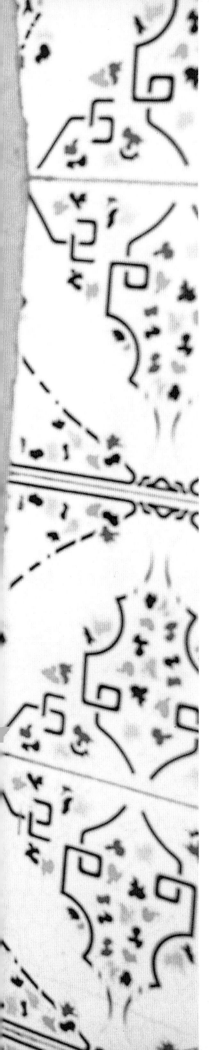

Moroccans prefer to complete a meal with fresh fruit, so there are very few traditional desserts or puddings. The only two of note served in the home are rice pudding and *mulhalabia*, an almond cream pudding. Yogurt, of course, is another "dessert," but the Moroccans only eat it mixed with sugar or honey—it is not used in other dishes. However, when fruit is served at banquets, some cooks are imaginative in their presentation, using orange flower water and rosewater to good effect, with a sprinkling of almonds, walnuts, or mint leaves. Fresh figs, watermelon, oranges, bananas, and peaches can look quite festive and the extra touches turn the fruit into tempting desserts.

Moroccan pastries have links to those of the Middle East, but are completely different in their final form. The *ghoriba* is a cookie you will find from the Middle East to Morocco in various forms, but Moroccans make baklava-type pastries their way—unique and just as delicious.

The similarities as far as pastries are concerned are in the ingredients used. Almonds feature prominently, especially ground almonds. Powdered sugar, cinnamon, orange flower water, rosewater, a hint of lemon zest, honey—these are the popular additives for making many of them. Walnuts, dates, dried figs, sesame seeds, and, to a lesser extent, pistachio nuts are also used according to the whim of the cook or the art of the pâtissier.

Fruit and almonds also feature in *sharbats*, sublime concoctions mixed with milk. Almond sharbat flavored with rosewater is a favorite; apple, raisin, strawberry, and avocado sharbats are also common. Aromatic flower waters or a dusting of ground cinnamon flavor fruit juices (orange, grape, pomegranate, and watermelon)—so Moroccan in concept. These drinks are of great importance, as the Koran forbids alcohol.

One beverage that was introduced from Arabia centuries ago is water perfumed with fragrant fumes. Grains of gum arabic are thrown on the embers of a charcoal grill and an unglazed pottery water jug is inverted over the fragrant smoke and is impregnated with the fumes. When the porous jug is filled with water, the water cools by evaporation and absorbs the fragrance. Unfortunately, with the availability of bottled mineral water, few Moroccans prepare it today.

However, none of these beverages come even close to mint tea in popularity—its supremacy is assured.

honey-dipped briouats
with almond paste .... makes 18

THESE CRISP, HONEY-DIPPED PASTRIES ARE FILLED WITH A DELICIOUS ALMOND PASTE FRAGRANT WITH ORANGE FLOWER WATER. WHEN BOILING HONEY FOR DIPPING, IT IS IMPORTANT TO ADD WATER, OTHERWISE THE HONEY BURNS. YOU MAY NEED TO ADD MORE WATER BEFORE DIPPING IS COMPLETED.

ground almonds	2 cups
unsalted butter	6 tablespoons
confectioners' sugar	1/2 cup
almond extract	1/4 teaspoon
orange flower water	3 tablespoons
phyllo pastry	6 sheets
smen	1/2 cup, melted
honey	3/4 cup

Heat a heavy-based saucepan, add the ground almonds, and stir constantly until lightly roasted—about 3–4 minutes. Tip immediately into a bowl, add the butter, and stir until melted. When cool, add the confectioners' sugar, almond extract, and 4 teaspoons of the orange flower water. Mix thoroughly to a paste.

Stack the phyllo sheets on a cutting board with the longer side toward you. Using a ruler and sharp knife, measure and cut the phyllo into strips 5 inches wide and 11–12 inches long. Stack the strips in the folds of a dry dish towel or cover them with plastic wrap to prevent them from drying out. You will need eighteen strips.

Place a phyllo strip on the work surface, brush half the length with smen, and fold it in half to give a strip 2 1/2 inches wide. Brush over the top with smen and place 1 tablespoon of the almond filling toward the end of the strip. Fold the end diagonally across the filling so that the base lines up with the side of the strip, forming a triangle. Fold straight up once, then fold diagonally to the opposite side. Continue folding in the same manner to the end of the strip, trimming any excess pastry with scissors. Place seam side down on a lightly greased cookie sheet. Repeat with the remaining ingredients. When completed, brush the tops lightly with smen.

Preheat the oven to 350°F. It is best to do this after the triangles are completed so that the kitchen remains cool during shaping. Bake the pastries for 20–25 minutes or until they are puffed and lightly golden.

Combine the honey, 1/4 cup water, and the remaining orange flower water in a 6-cup saucepan. Just before the pastries are removed from the oven, bring the honey to a boil, and then reduce the heat to low. Put two hot pastries at a time in the boiling honey, leave for 20 seconds, and then remove with two forks to a tray lined with waxed paper. Dip the remaining pastries in the same way, placing them on the tray right side up. As the pastries are dipped, the honey boils up in the pan, so be careful. Cool and serve on the day of baking.

Fold the end of the phyllo over the filling to form a triangle.

Put the hot pastries in the boiling honey for 20 seconds.

fried honey cakes .... serves 4–6

WHILE YEAST DOUGHS ARE USUALLY PREPARED FOR SWEETS SUCH AS THESE DELICIOUS HONEY CAKES, HERE EGGS AND BAKING POWDER ARE USED TO GIVE THE DESIRED LIGHTNESS WITHOUT THE NEED FOR LENGTHY KNEADING OF THE DOUGH. ORANGE ZEST LENDS A TRULY MOROCCAN FLAVOR.

eggs	3
orange juice	1/4 cup
oil	1/4 cup
orange zest	4 teaspoons grated
superfine sugar	1/4 cup
all-purpose flour	2 1/3 cups plus 1/3 cup extra
baking powder	1 teaspoon
oil	for deep-frying

syrup

lemon juice	3 tablespoons
sugar	1 1/4 cups
honey	1/3 cup
orange zest	4 teaspoons grated

Whisk the eggs, orange juice, and oil together in a large bowl. Add the orange zest and sugar and whisk until frothy. Sift in the flour and baking powder and mix with a wooden spoon until smooth, but still a bit sticky. Cover and set aside for 1 hour.

To make the syrup, put 1 1/4 cups cold water with the lemon juice and sugar in a saucepan and heat, stirring until the sugar dissolves. Bring to a boil, then reduce the heat and simmer for 5 minutes. Add the honey and orange zest and simmer for an additional 5 minutes. Keep warm.

Sprinkle a little of the extra flour onto the dough and transfer it to a lightly floured surface. Work in just enough extra flour to make a dough that doesn't stick to your hands. Roll it out to a thickness of 1/4 inch. It will be very elastic, so keep rolling and resting it until it stops shrinking. Cut out round cakes with a 2-inch cookie cutter.

Heat the oil in a large, deep-sided frying pan to 325°F or until a cube of bread dropped into the oil browns in 20 seconds. Fry the cakes three or four at a time for 1 minute on each side or until puffed and golden. Remove with tongs and drain on paper towels.

Using tongs, dip each cake into the warm honey syrup, long enough for it to soak in. Transfer to a platter. Serve warm or cold.

Fry the honey cakes until they are puffed and golden.

the desert date

According to a Moroccan saying, date palms must have their heads in fire and their feet in water—the hot Moroccan sun brings the fruit to succulent sweetness, and groundwater nourishes their roots.

The date has sustained the desert nomads for countless centuries. It still sustains those who have not given up their traditional existence, and is just as important to villagers and city dwellers. For food on the move, the date is difficult to beat—an instant boost of energy with its high sugar content, and a little protein, vitamins, and minerals thrown in. Taking a year to mature, fresh dates make their appearance in the souks, or marketplaces, in December, arranged painstakingly in mini pyramids. Hues vary from light golden brown and red-brown to a rich chocolate. There are dates ready for eating immediately, dates for cooking, and dates to have on hand for snacking.

As well as its fruit, the date palm provides fronds, which are dried and used for baskets and table mats. The fiber from its bark is made into ropes, the pits of the fruit are used for fuel, and the trunk is used for timber. Date palms can produce fruit for sixty years; however, they can exceed 100 feet in height and are cut down when harvesting becomes too difficult. In the Erfoud oasis alone, one million date palms flourish, encompassing thirty varieties. The average annual yield is about 100 pounds of fruit per tree.

Muslims regard the date palm as the tree of life and it is easy to see why.

sesame cookies . . . . makes about 36

SESAME SEEDS STAR IN THESE DELICIOUS COOKIES. THEIR NUTTY FLAVOR IS ACCENTUATED WHEN ROASTED, BUT MAKE SURE THAT THE SEEDS DO NOT BURN. THEY CAN BE BOUGHT FROM PATISSERIES IN THE CITIES, TO BE TAKEN HOME OR TO A NEARBY CAFÉ TO BE ENJOYED WITH MINT TEA OR COFFEE.

sesame seeds	1 1/2 cups, plus 3–4 tablespoons extra
all-purpose flour	1 cup sifted
superfine sugar	3/4 cup
baking powder	1 1/2 teaspoons
eggs	2, beaten
orange flower water	4 teaspoons

Put the sesame seeds in a heavy-based saucepan and stir constantly over medium heat for about 7 minutes or until golden. Tip them immediately into a bowl and leave to cool. Put the flour in the same saucepan, stir constantly over medium heat for about 5 minutes or until lightly golden, and then transfer immediately to a mixing bowl.

When the sesame seeds are cool, put them in a blender and process until reduced almost to a powder (this is best done in two batches, as it is difficult to process the seeds efficiently in one batch). Some seeds should remain visible after processing. Add to the flour, along with the sugar and baking powder, and mix thoroughly. Make a well in the center and add the beaten eggs and orange flower water. Stir into the dry ingredients, then knead well until smooth.

Put the extra sesame seeds in a shallow dish. Line two cookie sheets with baking paper or grease them well with butter. Preheat the oven to 350°F.

Break off pieces of dough the size of walnuts and roll them into balls, oiling your hands lightly to prevent the dough from sticking. Press the balls in the sesame seeds and flatten slightly. Lift carefully so that the topping is not disturbed and place them sesame side up on the cookie sheets, spacing them 2 inches apart to allow for spreading. Bake for 15–20 minutes or until golden. Leave on the cookie sheets for 10 minutes before removing to a wire rack to cool. Store in an airtight container.

Stir the sesame seeds over medium heat until golden.

gazelle's horns .... makes about 30

THESE PRETTY ALMOND-FILLED PASTRIES ARE CALLED *KAAB EL GHZAL*. FOR A DIFFERENT FINISH, THEY ARE ALSO DIPPED, ONE AT A TIME WHILE HOT, INTO A BOWL OF ORANGE FLOWER WATER, THEN INTO ANOTHER BOWL OF POWDERED SUGAR.

pastry

all-purpose flour	2½ cups
butter	1½ tablespoons, melted
egg yolk	1
orange flower water	3 tablespoons

almond filling

ground almonds	3 cups
confectioners' sugar	¾ cup
orange flower water	4 teaspoons
egg white	1, lightly beaten
unsalted butter	3 tablespoons, melted
ground cinnamon	½ teaspoon
almond extract	¼ teaspoon
confectioners' sugar	to serve

To make the pastry, put the flour, butter, egg yolk, orange flower water, and ¼ cup cold water in a food processor. Process until the dough forms on the blades, adding a little more water if necessary. Process for 1 minute to make the dough elastic. Turn out onto the work surface and knead until smooth. Divide in half, wrap in plastic wrap, and allow to set for 20 minutes.

To make the almond filling, mix all the ingredients to form a stiff paste. Shape the filling into 30 balls, using 1 tablespoon of filling per ball. Oil your hands and roll each ball to form a torpedo shape 3 inches long, tapering slightly at each end. Place on waxed paper and set aside. Preheat the oven to 350°F.

Roll out one ball of dough on a lightly floured work surface to a 12 x 16-inch rectangle, with the longer side facing you. Lay three almond shapes across the pastry, 2 inches from the bottom edge, 1¼ inches from the sides, and about 2 inches apart. Lightly brush the pastry edge and between the filling with water. Turn the bottom edge of the pastry over the filling and press firmly around the filling to seal. Cut around the filling with a fluted pastry wheel, leaving a ¾-inch border. Place on a cookie sheet and gently bend upward on the filling side to form a crescent. Straighten the edge of the pastry with a knife and repeat this process until all the filling is used (reroll the pastry trimmings). Bake for 15 minutes or until lightly browned. Transfer to a wire rack and dust with sifted confectioners' sugar while hot.

Trim the edge of the pastry to give a straight edge.

Turn the bottom edge of the pastry over the almond shapes.

Use a pastry wheel to cut around the filling, leaving a border.

three ways with figs

EATING FRESH FIGS—PLUMP, PURPLE AND LUSCIOUS—IS ONE OF THE FINEST PLEASURES OF LATE SUMMER THROUGH AUTUMN. THE GREEN OR WINTER FIGS ARE JUST AS DELICIOUS IN LATE AUTUMN. MOROCCANS MAKE THE MOST OF FIGS IN SEASON, SERVING THEM AT THE END OF A MEAL AND USING DRIED FIGS FOR SNACKING OR AS ADDITIONS TO SWEET PASTRIES. WHILE YOGURT IS NOT USUALLY SERVED WITH FRUIT (MOROCCANS EAT IT SWEETENED WITH SUGAR OR HONEY), ITS SLIGHT TARTNESS COMPLEMENTS THE SWEETNESS OF FIGS.

figs with rosewater, almonds, and honey

Wash 12 fresh, purple-skinned figs gently and pat them dry with paper towels. Cut each fig into quarters, starting from the stem end and cutting almost to the base, then gently open out and put on a serving platter. Cover and chill in the refrigerator for 1 hour or until needed. Coarsely chop 1/3 cup lightly roasted blanched almonds. Carefully dribble about 1/4 teaspoon rosewater onto the exposed center of each fig and sprinkle 1 teaspoon of the chopped almonds into each. Drizzle 1–2 tablespoons honey over the nuts. Serve immediately. Serves 6.

poached figs with almonds and spices

Rinse 2 1/3 cups dried figs and place in a bowl with cold water to cover generously. Soak for 8 hours or until plump. Drain the soaking water into a saucepan. Insert a blanched almond into each fig from the base. Wrap 3 cloves, 3 bruised cardamom pods, and 1/2 teaspoon black peppercorns in a piece of muslin and tie securely. Add 1/2 cup sugar to the soaking liquid and cook over medium heat, stirring until the sugar has dissolved. Bring to a boil and add the bag of spices, the thinly peeled zest of 1/2 lemon, 1 cinnamon stick, and the figs. Return to a boil, then reduce the heat and simmer for 30 minutes or until tender. Transfer the figs to a serving dish with a slotted spoon and strain the syrup over them. Serve warm or chilled with thick yogurt. Serves 4–6.

figs with honeyed yogurt

Gently wash 12 fresh figs and pat dry with paper towels. Chill for 30 minutes. Mix 1 cup plain yogurt with 3 tablespoons honey. Coarsely chop 3 tablespoons pistachio nuts and set aside. Cut each fig into quarters, starting from the stem end and cutting almost to the base. Gently open each fig and place on a flat serving dish. Dribble 1/4 teaspoon orange flower water over the exposed center of each fig and pile about 4 teaspoons of the yogurt into each. Drizzle 1 teaspoon honey on top of the yogurt and sprinkle with the chopped pistachios. Serves 4–6.

ghoriba

GHORIBA ARE BAKED IN THE MIDDLE EAST AND MOROCCO. INGREDIENTS VARY A LITTLE; THIS MOROCCAN VERSION USES VERY FINE SEMOLINA AS WELL AS FLOUR, BUT YOU CAN USE ANY FLOUR IF THE REQUIRED SEMOLINA IS UNAVAILABLE.

unsalted butter	1 cup
all-purpose flour	1 cup
confectioners' sugar	1 cup, plus extra to serve, optional
very fine semolina	2 cups
eggs	2, beaten
natural vanilla extract	1 teaspoon
egg white	1, lightly beaten
blanched almonds	¼ cup, split

Melt the butter in a heavy-based saucepan over low heat. Skim off the froth, then pour into a mixing bowl, leaving the white milk solids in the pan. Set aside to cool.

Sift the flour and sugar into a bowl, add the semolina and a pinch of salt, and mix thoroughly. When the butter is cool but still liquid, stir in the egg and vanilla. Add the dry ingredients and mix to a firm dough, adding more flour if necessary. Knead well, then cover with plastic wrap and allow to sit for 1 hour. Line two cookie sheets with baking paper. Preheat the oven to 350°F.

Knead the dough again until smooth and pliant. Shape 1 tablespoon of the dough into a smooth ball, then shape the remaining dough into balls of the same size. Place on the prepared cookie sheets 1 inch apart. Brush the tops lightly with egg white and press an almond on top of each cookie. Bake for 20 minutes or until lightly golden. Cool on the cookie sheets. When cool, dust the cookies with sifted confectioners' sugar, if desired, and store in an airtight container.

Semolina is the milled inner endosperm of hard or durum wheat, and is pale beige or yellow in color and granular in appearance. It can be very fine (almost like a flour), fine, or coarse, the latter used to manufacture couscous, although fine semolina is also used for a fine-grained couscous not readily available outside Morocco. Both fine and coarse semolina are sold as breakfast cereals. Very fine semolina is available at markets selling Middle Eastern and Greek foods. Semolina flour, used in pasta making, is durum wheat flour and should not be confused with the semolina described above.

almond macaroons..makes 30–35

THESE ALMOND COOKIES ARE DIPPED INTO POWDERED SUGAR BEFORE BAKING. DURING BAKING, THEY RISE A LITTLE AND THE SUGAR TOPPING DEVELOPS A LOVELY CRACKED APPEARANCE. MOROCCAN COOKS TAKE THESE COOKIES TO THE COMMUNAL OVEN FOR BAKING, TO BE ENJOYED LATER WITH MINT TEA.

ground almonds	3 cups
confectioners' sugar	1 1/4 cups plus 1/4 cup extra
baking powder	1 1/2 teaspoons
ground cinnamon	1/2 teaspoon
egg	1
lemon zest	2 teaspoons grated
rosewater	4 teaspoons

Put the ground almonds in a mixing bowl and sift in the sugar, baking powder, and cinnamon. Stir well to mix the dry ingredients thoroughly. Beat the egg with the lemon zest and rosewater and add to the dry ingredients. Mix to a firm paste and knead lightly.

Line two cookie sheets with baking paper. Sift the extra sugar into a shallow dish. Preheat the oven to 350°F.

Break off pieces of dough the size of walnuts and roll into balls, oiling your hands lightly to prevent the dough from sticking. Press the balls into the confectioners' sugar and flatten them slightly. Lift carefully so that the topping is not disturbed and place on the cookie sheets sugar side up, spacing them about 2 inches apart to allow for spreading. Bake for 20 minutes. Leave the macaroons on the cookie sheets for 10 minutes before removing to a wire rack to cool. Store in an airtight container.

Mix the almond mixture to a firm paste and knead lightly.

Press the balls of dough into the confectioners' sugar.

three ways with flower waters

ONE OF THE DEFINING CHARACTERISTICS OF MOROCCAN COOKING IS THE USE OF FRAGRANT WATERS IN SAVORY AND SWEET DISHES. KNOWN AS *MA'EL WARD*, ROSEWATER IS A DISTILLATION OF ROSE PETALS AND ORIGINATED IN PERSIA; IN MOROCCO, IT IS DISTILLED FROM ROSEBUDS COLLECTED IN THE VALLEY OF DADES. ORANGE FLOWER WATER IS KNOWN AS *ZHAAR*, AND IS A DISTILLATION OF THE BLOSSOMS OF THE BITTER *BIGARADE* OR SEVILLE ORANGE; IT ORIGINATED IN THE MIDDLE EAST. BOTH WATERS WERE INTRODUCED TO MOROCCO BY THE ARABS.

grape juice with rosewater

Wash 1 lb. 2 oz. chilled seedless purple or green grapes very well. Drain them and cut off the thicker stalks, leaving the grapes in small bunches. Feed the grapes into a juice extractor, catching the juice in a pitcher. When all the grapes are juiced, let the juice settle and then skim off any dark froth (this is the remnants of the stems and seeds). Cover the pitcher with plastic wrap and chill in the refrigerator for at least 1 hour. Pour the juice into two tall glasses, leaving any sediment in the pitcher. Stir ½ teaspoon rosewater into each glass and dust the top lightly with ground cinnamon if desired. Serves 2.

watermelon juice with rosewater

Chill 1 lb. 12 oz. watermelon thoroughly. Remove the rind and cut the pink part only into thick chunks that will fit into a juice extractor feed tube. Extract the juice into a pitcher. Be careful when extracting the juice, as the seeds have a tendency to jump out of the feed tube. Add 1 teaspoon rosewater and pour into two tall glasses, or store in the pitcher in the refrigerator until ready to serve. Serves 2.

orange juice with orange flower water

Choose 6 sweet oranges and store them in the refrigerator so they are well chilled. Using a citrus juicer, juice the oranges and pour the juice through a sieve into a pitcher. Stir in superfine sugar to taste (you may not need to add any sugar at all if the oranges are very sweet), and add 1½ teaspoons orange flower water. Pour into two tall glasses and lightly dust the top with ground cinnamon if desired. Serve immediately. Serves 2.

almond phyllo snake .... serves 8

THIS COILED PASTRY—CALLED *M'HANNCHA* IN MOROCCO—WITH ITS FRAGRANT ALMOND FILLING IS ONE OF MOROCCO'S MOST FAMOUS PASTRIES. SERVE IT IN WEDGES OR BREAK OFF PIECES FROM THE COIL AS THEY DO IN MOROCCO. EITHER WAY, SERVE WITH MINT TEA OR COFFEE.

egg	1 small, separated
ground almonds	2 cups
flaked almonds	1/3 cup
confectioners' sugar	1 cup, plus extra to serve
lemon zest	1 teaspoon finely grated
almond extract	1/4 teaspoon
rosewater	4 teaspoons
unsalted butter or smen	6 tablespoons, melted
phyllo pastry	8–9 sheets
ground cinnamon	a pinch

Preheat the oven to 350°F. Lightly grease an 8-inch round cake pan.

Put the egg white in a bowl and beat lightly with a fork. Add the ground almonds, flaked almonds, confectioners' sugar, lemon zest, almond extract, and rosewater. Mix to a paste.

Divide the almond mixture into four portions. Roll each portion on a cutting board into a sausage shape about 1/2 inch thick and about 2 inches shorter than the length of the phyllo. If the paste is too sticky to roll, dust the board with confectioners' sugar.

Keep the melted butter or smen warm by placing the saucepan in another pan filled with hot water. Remove one sheet of phyllo pastry and place the rest in the folds of a dry dish towel or cover them with plastic wrap to prevent them from drying out. Brush the phyllo sheet with the butter, then cover with another sheet, brushing the top with butter. Ease one almond "sausage" off the board onto the buttered pastry, laying it along the length of the pastry, 1 inch from the base and sides. Roll up to enclose the filling. Form into a coil and set the coil seam side down in the center of the prepared pan, tucking under the unfilled ends of the pastry to enclose the filling. Continue in this manner to make more pastry "snakes," shaping them to make a large coil. If the coil breaks, cut small pieces of the remaining phyllo sheet, brush with a little egg yolk, and press the phyllo onto the breaks.

Add the cinnamon to the remaining egg yolk and brush over the coil. Bake for 30–35 minutes or until golden brown. Dust with the extra confectioners' sugar and serve warm. This sweet pastry can be stored at room temperature for up to two days.

Roll the phyllo pastry around the almond filling.

Fit the coils into the tin, tucking under the ends.

keneffa . . . . serves 6

IN MOROCCO, FRIED *WARKHA* PASTRY IS USED FOR THIS TRADITIONAL DESSERT. ASSEMBLED IN A STACK OF LARGE ROUNDS LAYERED WITH ALMOND CREAM AND ALMONDS, IT COLLAPSES INTO A CRUMBLED MASS ONCE PORTIONS ARE TAKEN FROM IT. MAKING INDIVIDUAL PASTRY STACKS USING WONTON WRAPPERS SOLVES THIS PROBLEM.

almond cream

whole milk	3 cups
cornstarch	1/4 cup
sugar	1/4 cup
ground almonds	1/2 cup
almond extract	1/4 teaspoon
rosewater	2 tablespoons
blanched almonds	2/3 cup, lightly roasted
confectioners' sugar	3 tablespoons sifted, plus extra to serve
ground cinnamon	1/2 teaspoon
square wonton wrappers	40
oil	for frying
organic rose petals	to serve

To make the almond cream, put 1/2 cup of the milk in a large bowl, add the cornstarch, and mix to a thin paste. Bring the remaining milk to a boil until it froths up. Mix the cornstarch paste again and add the boiling milk, mixing constantly with a whisk. Pour this back into the saucepan and stir in the sugar and ground almonds. Return to the heat and stir constantly with a wooden spoon until thickened and bubbling. Reduce the heat and boil gently for 1 minute. Pour the liquid back into the bowl and stir in the almond extract and rosewater. Press a piece of plastic wrap on the surface and leave to cool. Just before using the cream, stir briskly with a whisk to smooth it; if it is too thick, stir in a little milk to give a pouring consistency.

Coarsely chop the roasted almonds, mix with the confectioners' sugar and cinnamon, and set aside.

Bring the wonton wrappers to room temperature. Lightly brush a wrapper with water and press another firmly on top. Repeat until there are eighteen pairs. Make two extra pairs in case some are burned during frying.

In a large frying pan, add oil to a depth of 1/2 inch and place over high heat. When the oil is hot but not smoking, reduce the heat to medium and add two pairs of wonton wrappers. Fry quickly for about 20 seconds until lightly browned, turning to brown evenly. Using tongs, remove the wrappers and drain on paper towels. Repeat with the remaining squares.

To assemble the pastries, put a fried pastry square in the center of each plate. Drizzle with a little almond cream and sprinkle with a heaping teaspoon of the chopped almond mixture. Repeat with another pastry square, cream, and almonds. Finish with another pastry square. Sprinkle with pink rose petals from organic roses. Sift a little confectioners' sugar on the top and serve with the remaining almond cream.

Brush a wrapper with water and then press another on top.

Fry the pairs of wonton wrappers until lightly browned.

three ways with almonds

ALMONDS GROW PROLIFICALLY IN MOROCCO AND SO ARE WIDELY USED IN COOKING. THE BLANCHED NUTS ARE ROASTED AND SPRINKLED OVER TAGINES, POUNDED AND MADE INTO FRAGRANT PASTES FOR PASTRY FILLINGS, ADDED TO DESSERTS SUCH AS *MULHALABIA* (ALMOND CREAM PUDDING), AND MADE INTO LIP-SMACKING *SHARBAT BIL LOOZ* (ALMOND SHARBAT). IN THE SOUTH, *AMALOU* (ALMOND AND HONEY SPREAD) IS A DELICIOUS SPREAD FOR BREAD OR PANCAKES. ARGAN OIL, FROM THE ARGAN TREE, IS TRADITIONALLY USED, BUT OTHER NUT OILS ARE FINE.

almond sharbat

Put 1 1/2 cups blanched almonds and 1/4 cup superfine sugar in a blender with 1 cup water. Blend until the almonds are well pulverized. Line a strainer with a double layer of cheesecloth, place over a bowl, and pour the almond mixture into the strainer. Add 1/4 cup water to the blender and blend briefly to clean the blender of any almond residue. Pour into the strainer. Press the almonds to extract as much moisture as possible, gather up the cheesecloth, twist the end, and squeeze firmly over the bowl, making sure that the almonds are safely enclosed. Put the cheesecloth and almonds in the strainer again, add another 1/4 cup water, stir, and squeeze the almonds again. Discard the almonds. Stir in 1/4 teaspoon almond extract, 1/2 teaspoon rosewater, and 1 cup milk. Taste and add a little more sugar if necessary. Chill and serve. (If you can find them, float a fragrant pink rose petal or two on top of each sharbat, but make sure the petals are free of pesticides.) Serves 4.

almond cream pudding

Put 2 cups milk and 1/4 cup superfine sugar in a heavy-based saucepan and heat over medium heat until the sugar has dissolved. Bring to a boil. In a large bowl, mix 3 tablespoons cornstarch, 4 teaspoons ground rice, and 1/4 cup water to a smooth paste. Pour in the boiling milk, stirring constantly with a whisk. Return to the saucepan and stir over medium heat until thickened and bubbling. Add 2/3 cup ground almonds and simmer over low heat for 5 minutes, stirring occasionally. Add 1 teaspoon rosewater and remove the pan from the heat. Stir occasionally to cool a little, then spoon into serving bowls. Refrigerate for 1 hour. Mix 3 tablespoons roasted, slivered (or flaked) almonds with 1 teaspoon superfine sugar and 1/2 teaspoon ground cinnamon and sprinkle on the top before serving. Serves 4.

almond and honey spread

Put 1 cup ground almonds, a pinch of salt, and 3 tablespoons walnut or macadamia nut oil in a bowl and stir well. Mix in 4 teaspoons dark honey and 3–4 drops almond extract. The *amalou* should have a soft, spreading consistency; if necessary, stir in a little more oil. The amount of oil required depends on the moistness of the ground almonds. Serve the spread on bread, semolina pancakes (page 176), or other pancakes, with additional honey if desired. The amalou can be stored in a sealed jar in the refrigerator for three to four weeks; bring to room temperature before serving. Makes 1/2 cup.

semolina pancakes ....

THE RESEMBLANCE TO ENGLISH CRUMPETS IS APPARENT, BUT ONCE TASTED, THERE IS NO COMPARISON. THESE LIGHT-AS-AIR PANCAKES ARE MADE WITH FLOUR AND VERY FINE SEMOLINA, RESULTING IN PANCAKES THAT BEG FOR LASHINGS OF BUTTER AND HONEY.

active dried yeast	4 teaspoons
all-purpose flour	2 cups
very fine semolina	1²/₃ cups
eggs	2
milk	¹/₂ cup, lukewarm
oil	for cooking
unsalted butter	to serve
honey	warm, to serve

Dissolve the yeast in ¹/₂ cup lukewarm water. Mix in 1 tablespoon of the flour, cover with a cloth, and leave in a warm place for 15 minutes until frothy.

Sift the remaining flour, semolina, and ¹/₂ teaspoon salt into a mixing bowl and make a well in the center. Beat the eggs lightly with the lukewarm milk and pour into the flour mixture, then add the yeast mixture and 1¹/₂ cups lukewarm water. Starting with the flour surrounding the well and working outward, bring the flour into the liquid, then beat well with a whisk for 5–7 minutes until smooth, adding more water if necessary. The batter should have the consistency of heavy cream. Cover the bowl with a folded dish towel and leave in a warm place for 1 hour until bubbles form and the batter doubles in bulk.

Fill a saucepan one-third full with water, bring to a simmer, then place a large heatproof plate over the top. Put a dish towel, folded into quarters, on the plate.

Heat a heavy cast-iron frying pan or crepe pan over high heat. Reduce the heat to medium and rub the pan with a wad of paper towels dipped in oil. Pour in a small ladleful of batter, about ¹/₄ cup, and, using the bottom of the ladle, quickly shape into a round about 6 inches in diameter. Work quickly and try to make the top as even as possible. Cook until the top of the pancake looks dry and is peppered with little holes from the bubbles. While it is not traditional, you can turn it over and briefly brown the bubbly side.

Remove the pancake to the folds of the dish towel, bubbly side up, and cover to keep warm. Overlap the pancakes rather than stack them. Repeat with the remaining batter, oiling the pan with the wad of paper towels between each pancake. Serve the pancakes hot with butter and warm honey.

Use the bottom of the ladle to shape the batter into a round.

Cook the pancake until the top is peppered with little holes.

moroccan doughnuts................................makes 20

ALL OVER MOROCCO YOU WILL FIND DOUGHNUT MAKERS, WITH CAULDRONS OF HOT OIL, FRYING DOUGHNUTS TO ORDER. THESE ARE STRUNG ON LENGTHS OF PALM FRONDS AND TIED, TO BE TAKEN HOME OR TO A CAFÉ, WHERE THEY WILL BE DIPPED IN SUGAR AND ENJOYED WITH MINT TEA.

active dried yeast	2 teaspoons
sugar	1/2 teaspoon
all-purpose flour	3 cups
oil	for deep-frying
superfine sugar	to serve
ground cinnamon	to serve, optional

Dissolve the yeast in 1/2 cup lukewarm water and stir in the sugar. Combine the flour and 1/2 teaspoon salt in a shallow mixing bowl and make a well in the center. Pour the yeast mixture into the well and add another 1/2 cup lukewarm water. Stir sufficient flour into the liquid to form a thin batter, cover the bowl with a cloth, and leave for 15 minutes until bubbles form. Gradually stir in the remaining flour, then mix with your hand to form a soft dough. If it is too stiff, add a little more water, 1 teaspoon at a time. Knead for 5 minutes in the bowl until smooth and elastic. Pour a little oil down the side of the bowl, turn the dough to coat with oil, cover with a cloth, and leave for 1 hour until doubled in bulk.

Punch down the dough, then turn it out onto the work surface and divide into twenty equal portions. With lightly oiled hands, roll each into a smooth ball. Brush a cookie sheet with oil. Using your index finger, punch a hole in the center of one dough ball, then twirl it on your finger until the hole enlarges to 3/4 inch in diameter. Place on the sheet. Repeat with the remaining balls.

Fill a large saucepan one-third full of oil and heat to 375°F or until a cube of bread dropped in the oil browns in 10 seconds. Have a long metal skewer on hand and begin with the first doughnut that was shaped. Drop the doughnut into the oil, immediately put the skewer in the center, and twirl it around in a circular motion for 2–3 seconds to keep the hole open. Fry for 1 1/2–2 minutes or until the doughnut is evenly browned. Once this process is mastered, drop two to three doughnuts at a time into the oil, briefly twirling the skewer in the center of the first before adding the next. When cooked, put the skewer in the doughnut hole and lift it out onto a tray lined with paper towels.

Toss the doughnuts in sugar and eat while warm with coffee or mint tea. While it is not traditional in Morocco, cinnamon may be mixed with the sugar and sprinkled on top.

Twirl the doughnut in a circular motion to keep the hole open.

three ways with fresh fruit

IN EVERY MOROCCAN HOUSEHOLD, THE MAIN MEAL IS COMPLETED WITH FRESH FRUIT, EITHER PICKED FROM COURTYARD FRUIT TREES OR BOUGHT AT THE SOUK. AT BANQUETS, BEAUTIFULLY ARRANGED PLATTERS OF FRESH FRUIT, OFTEN NESTLED IN ICE, CELEBRATE THE SEASON. WHEN FRUIT IS PREPARED, IT CAN BE SCENTED WITH FLOWER WATER, DUSTED WITH CINNAMON, AND CROWNED WITH CHOPPED NUTS—A VISUAL AND SENSORY DELIGHT AND THE PERFECT FINALE TO A MEAL.

watermelon with rosewater and mint

Wipe the skin of a 3 lb. 5 oz. piece of watermelon with a clean, damp cloth. Working over a plate to catch any juice, remove the skin and cut the watermelon into 1 1/4-inch cubes, removing any visible seeds. Pile the cubes in a bowl or on a platter. Pour the watermelon juice into a small pitcher and stir in 1 tablespoon rosewater. Sprinkle over the watermelon, cover, and chill in the refrigerator for 1 hour or until ready to serve. Sprinkle with small fresh mint leaves and serve chilled. Serves 4.

peaches with sugar and cinnamon

Peel 6 freestone peaches. To do this, cut around each peach following the groove on the side of the peach. Put the peaches in a bowl of boiling water for 1 minute, then plunge them into a bowl of cold water to cool. Remove from the water and peel the skin away—it should slip off easily. Separate the peach halves with a gentle twist and remove the pits. Brush the cut surfaces lightly with lemon juice. Set the peach halves on a bed of crushed ice in a large, shallow bowl. Crush 4 sugar cubes, sprinkle on each peach half, and dust lightly with ground cinnamon. Serves 4.

bananas with yogurt

Slice 4–5 large bananas at an angle to give longish ovals of banana about 1 1/2 inches thick. Arrange in overlapping circles in a round, shallow dish. Mix 1/4 cup fresh orange juice with 1 tablespoon orange flower water and sprinkle over the banana. Mix 1 cup plain yogurt with 3 tablespoons honey and pile in the center of the banana. Lightly roast and chop 1/2 cup walnut pieces and sprinkle over the yogurt and banana. Drizzle 4 teaspoons thick honey over the walnuts. Serves 4.

briouats with dates and figs

FOR THESE PASTRIES, USE THE SOFTER DESSERT FIGS OR, IF ONLY DRIED FIGS ARE AVAILABLE, PICK OUT THE SOFTER ONES. IF DESIRED, ONLY DATES MAY BE USED WITH THE ALMONDS, BUT THE COMBINATION OF FRUITS MAKES THESE ALL THE MORE ENJOYABLE.

smen or butter	1/2 cup melted
blanched almonds	1 cup
dates	1/2 cup chopped and pitted
dessert figs (soft, dried figs)	1/2 cup chopped
orange flower water	4 teaspoons
phyllo pastry	12–14 sheets
confectioners' sugar	to serve

In a small frying pan, warm 4 teaspoons of the smen or butter, add the almonds, and cook over medium heat until golden, stirring often. Tip immediately into a food processor, along with the smen in the pan. When the almonds are cool, process until finely chopped. Then add the dates, figs, and orange flower water and process to a thick paste, scraping down the side of the bowl as necessary. Rub your hands with a little of the smen, place the paste onto the work surface, and gather it into a ball. Roll into a sausage shape 9 inches long and cut it into eighteen equal pieces. Roll each piece into a cigar shape 4 inches long. Place on a sheet of waxed paper and set aside.

Count out 12 sheets of phyllo pastry (if the pastry is shorter than 15 1/2 inches in length, you will need extra sheets). Stack the phyllo on a cutting surface. Using a ruler and sharp knife, measure and cut across the width through the stack to give strips 5 inches wide and about 11–12 inches long. Stack the cut phyllo in the folds of a dry dish towel or cover with plastic wrap to prevent it from drying out.

Place a strip of pastry with the narrow end nearest you and brush with the melted smen. Top with another strip of pastry and brush with melted smen. Put the shaped filling 1/2 inch from the base and 1/2 inch from the sides of the strip. Fold the end of the phyllo over the filling, fold in the sides, and brush the side folds with smen. Roll to the end and place seam side down on a greased cookie sheet. Repeat with the remaining ingredients. Preheat the oven to 350°F after the *briouats* are completed to keep the kitchen cool while shaping.

Brush the tops of the *briouats* lightly with smen and bake in the preheated oven for 20 minutes or until lightly golden. Sift confectioners' sugar over them while they are still hot. When cool, store in a sealed container. The rolls keep for two days when stored at room temperature.

Roll each piece of the paste into a short cigar shape.

Put the filling at the bottom of the strip and fold the phyllo over it.

mint tea

Mint grows abundantly in Morocco and was favored as a tisane in the past. With the opportune introduction of green tea in the 1850s, Moroccans discovered the two ingredients were made for each other. Spearmint (*Mentha spicata* or *M. viridis*) is the preferred mint and the preferred tea is green gunpowder or, more specifically, Formosan Gunpowder tea.

Put the tea in a warmed teapot, with the amount varying according to the maker's tastes—about 4 teaspoons is normal. Pour in boiling water, leave to brew for a minute or so, and then add 1–3 tablespoons sugar and a good handful of well-washed, leafy mint stalks. Brew for 3 minutes. Pour the tea into tea glasses with a sprig of mint. The mint in the teapot acts as a strainer for the tea leaves.

In Morocco, tea is usually sweetened generously with highly refined loaf sugar; this is shaped in cones about 8 inches high and wrapped in purple paper (or plastic); the amount needed is broken off by the tea maker using a special silver hammer. The teapot—like the British "Manchester" with a bulbous body and domed lid—is made in silver plate, aluminum, or stainless steel. Tea is poured from a height to aerate it, and is sometimes poured from two teapots for maximum effect and aeration—guests are expected to have three glasses. And how do you drink hot tea from a glass? Grip the rim of the glass with the thumb and forefinger of the right hand and sip.

date candies .... serves 6–8

THE BERBERS, ESPECIALLY NOMADIC TRIBES, DEPENDED HEAVILY ON THE DATE AS A FOOD. DATES ARE USED WIDELY IN THEIR COOKING AND ARE MADE INTO SWEETMEATS WITH A RANGE OF INGREDIENTS. THE INCLUSION OF SMEN AND NUTS INCREASES THE ENERGY VALUE OF THIS PARTICULAR SWEETMEAT.

walnut halves	1½ cups
sesame seeds	3 tablespoons
smen or ghee	½ cup
pitted dried dates	4 cups, coarsely chopped

Preheat the oven to 350°F and line the base of a small square pan with waxed paper. Spread the walnuts on a baking sheet and bake for 5 minutes or until lightly roasted. Chop coarsely. Bake the sesame seeds on a baking sheet until golden.

Melt the smen or ghee in a large heavy-based saucepan and cook the dates, covered, over low heat for about 10 minutes, stirring often until the dates soften. Using the back of a spoon dipped in cold water, spread half the dates over the base of the prepared pan. Sprinkle the walnuts on top and press into the dates. Spread the remaining dates over the walnuts. Smooth the surface with wet fingers and press down firmly.

Sprinkle with the sesame seeds and press lightly into the dates. When cool, remove the set mixture from the pan and cut into small diamonds to serve.

To make smen (clarified butter), cut 1 cup salted or unsalted butter into pieces and put in a small, heavy-based saucepan over low heat, using a heat diffuser if necessary to prevent the butter from spitting. Simmer very gently for 25 minutes or until the milk solids brown very lightly. Pour the hot butter through a muslin-lined strainer set over a bowl. The clear oil is the smen. It will have a slightly nutty taste. Herbed smen can be made by putting some *za'atar* (a wild thymelike herb) and salt into the strainer and pouring the hot butter oil through this to flavor it. Store smen in a sealed jar in the refrigerator. Ghee is a good substitute.

rice pudding with raisins . . . . serves 8

THIS IS SERVED IN A COMMUNAL DISH IN MOROCCAN HOUSEHOLDS AND EATEN WITH A SPOON. THE TOPPING CAN VARY—USUALLY DABS OF BUTTER ARE PLACED ON THE WARM PUDDING, BUT A FESTIVE FLAIR CAN BE ACHIEVED BY ADDING CHOPPED TOASTED ALMONDS, OR RAISINS AND HONEY AS IN THE RECIPE BELOW.

short-grain rice	1/2 cup
milk	41/2 cups
sugar	1/4 cup
ground almonds	1/2 cup
cornstarch	3 tablespoons
almond extract	1/4 teaspoon
orange flower water	3 tablespoons
raisins	3 tablespoons
honey	3 tablespoons

Put the rice in a large heavy-based saucepan with a pinch of salt and 1 cup water. Cook over medium heat for 5 minutes, stirring occasionally until the water has been absorbed.

Set aside 1/2 cup of the milk. Stir 1 cup of the remaining milk into the rice and bring to a simmer. When the rice has absorbed the milk, add another 1 cup milk. Continue to cook the rice until all the milk has been added, ensuring each addition of milk is absorbed before adding the next. (Adding the milk gradually helps prevent the milk from boiling over.) The rice should be very soft in 30 minutes, with the final addition of milk barely absorbed.

Mix the sugar with the ground almonds and break up any lumps. Stir this into the rice mixture and simmer gently for 2–3 minutes. Mix the cornstarch with the reserved milk and stir into the rice. When thickened, boil gently for 2 minutes. Remove the pan from the heat and stir in the almond extract and 2 tablespoons of the orange flower water. Stir the pudding occasionally to cool it a little.

Meanwhile, steep the raisins in the remaining orange flower water for 15 minutes. Pour the pudding into a serving bowl. When a slight skin forms on the top, sprinkle with the soaked raisins and drizzle with the honey. Cool completely before serving in individual bowls.

Cook the rice, stirring occasionally until the water is absorbed.

Gradually add the milk to the rice and cook until absorbed.

index

Thunder Bay Press
An imprint of the Advantage Publishers Group
5880 Oberlin Drive, San Diego, CA 92121-4794
www.thunderbaybooks.com

All notations of errors or omissions should be addressed to Thunder Bay Press, Editorial Department, at the above address. All other correspondence (author inquiries, permissions) concerning the content of this book should be addressed to Murdoch Books Pty Limited, Pier 8/9 23 Hickson Road, Millers Point NSW 2000, Australia.

ISBN 1-59223-403-8
Library of Congress Cataloging-in-Publication Data available upon request.

Printed in China.
1 2 3 4 5   09 08 07 06 05

IMPORTANT: Those who might be at risk from the effects of salmonella poisoning (the elderly, pregnant women, young children, and those suffering from immune deficiency diseases) should consult their doctor with any concerns about eating raw eggs.